MURDER

IS A FAMILY AFFAIR

Donalie Beltran

Murder Is A Family Affair
Copyright © 2013 Donalie T Beltran

After many years of research, all known information concerning these members of the Tuxhorn family is included to the best of the author's knowledge at the time of writing. Author is not responsible for new or contradicting information, should any occur, now or at a later date.

Additional information: MurderIsAFamilyAffair.com

ISBN: 0989636208
ISBN-13: 9780989636209

This title will be available in ebook edition in Fall of 2014.

Cover design: Donalie Beltran
Cover photography, cowboy: iStockphoto®

Published by: Killing Time Press, LLC

ACKNOWLEDGEMENT

I thank my parents, Ray and Blanche Tuxhorn, for their support with this difficult family story. My husband, Bob, for his patience during this long process. I love you all.

Thanks to my cousin, Linda Hansel. Her Tuxhorn family tree provided me with valuable information. Contact Linda if you would like the genealogy book on the entire Tuxhorn family at lwhgeneo@sbcglobal.net.

Mostly, my thanks go to God, my Father in Heaven. I was adopted into His family through Jesus Christ and what He did on Calvary. I needed His strength and guidance to be able to tell the ugly truth without losing myself in it.

~ Donalie Beltran

PART ONE

AUGUST TUXHORN

CHAPTER ONE

He imagined it was a funeral much like any other, but what made this one different was the fact this grave would hold his headless father.

Standing around him were those who mourned, those who pretended to mourn, and, of course, the deceased. August couldn't help but notice the temperature was cold, even though the sun was shining brightly on this unusually quiet November morning.

When he thought about it, it seemed to be a perfect time of year for a funeral. November desperately clung to its past with autumn, but would soon fall to the demands of tomorrow's winter. Not unlike funerals—watching the past go away and being forced to face the future. He smiled at his own brilliant analogy. *Maybe I should be a poet!*

August Tüxhorn looked at the coffin sitting beside the grave, dug just yesterday. The coffin was nailed shut, but he knew who was inside. The dead, fifty-four year-old year old H. Henry Tüxhorn, was a muscular man with greying brown hair and small, acorn brown eyes. The 'H' stood for Herman, but the old man never used it. Scars from many fights could be found on each hand across the knuckles, as well as scars on his face received from those who didn't go down easily.

He lived in the small farming hamlet of Bielefeld in Westphalia, Prussia. At least he did until he decided to take his old shotgun and put it to use one more time. Alone in his field, he sat down on a rock and tied a long string to the shotgun's trigger. He then put the barrel under his chin and pulled the string. It was a less than dignified, albeit speedy, way to die.

The 'shotgun under the chin' thing was where he got the 'headless' part. Then add the four days the animals got to partake of him until he was found, and you had a much smaller casket than would normally be needed for Henry. August knew he shouldn't joke about it all, but he had to admit, it was pretty funny.

Strangely, he felt nothing at losing his father. That, in itself, was a surprise, considering father and son hated each other passionately.

August knew the Catholic priest presiding over the funeral would not waste any effort in extolling the decedent's endearing qualities. The simple fact of the matter was, the priest wouldn't be able to think of any. Not one.

Just as expected, the priest proceeded with the primary service in Latin and let it roll across the barren fields in his most powerful voice.

Hoc autem dico fratres quoniam caro et sanguis regnum Dei possidere non possunt neque corruptio incorruptelam possidebit...

Because a priest was present did not mean Henry was a religious man. Quite the contrary; he didn't believe in God at all. However, a priest was required to officiate due to the government and Catholicism being one and the same. August knew just being born in Westphalia, like he was, made a man Catholic. The thing that angered him the most was being involved in the Church was required by law. *Required by law!*

Giving most of what a man earned to the state was not considered being severely taxed, it was 'giving to God.' What a joke. It was just to line the pockets of a broke Church and crooked politicians. Not all Prussians were stupid enough to believe their garbage.

*...ecce mysterium vobis dico omnes quidem resurgemus
sed non omnes inmutabimur...*

He was irritated with his sandy, collar-length hair blowing in the cold breeze, while he had to hold his hat in his hand. Keeping his hair from blowing was what a hat was for, right? *Stupid religious rituals.* His coat kept him body warm, and his hat should have kept his head warm.

August rubbed at his full mustache, as he glanced over at his mother, Anna. Henry's abused and long-suffering wife was in quiet contemplation. She wore the only decent dress she owned, the same pale blue as her eyes, which now seemed clouded in thought.

The old coat she wore was actually Henry's, since he wouldn't let her spend frivolously on things she didn't need.

"Where was she going to go that she would need a coat? Her place is at home." August wondered what he would say now.

He imagined his mother was trying to adjust to the sudden change in her status over the past few days. A widow at forty-five, she was now in charge of her own life and that of the children still at home. He wondered how she would handle it. But then, truth be told, he was not sure he really cared. Women and their perceived problems were nothing but a bane for a man. They were hard to tolerate.

The wind was picking up as August continued to let his eyes roam. He felt a small shiver from the cold. All eleven children, ranging from twenty-seven down to ten years of age, were present and stood about the gravesite lost in their own thoughts. Like everyone else, they only half listened to the undecipherable Latin requiem.

Those present might not admit it, but August knew each was silently pleased the old man was gone, no matter how distasteful the way it happened. Only seven of the children were still living at home. At twenty-two, he was one of them. The older siblings were married and had built homes in the community and still farmed the area.

> *…in momento in ictu oculi in novissima tuba canet enim et mortui resurgent incorrupti et nos inmutabimur.*

His father left this life pretty much as he had lived it, in a violent rage. August knew Henry would be remembered as an evil man of short temper, who made those around him pay for his inability to control his own anger. His family fared the worst; August could attest to that. However, he knew the neighbors also quickly learned to keep their head down when Henry came strolling by.

Chancing a wrong look or misinterpreted nod; an unfortunate neighbor could be laid up for weeks trying to heal from a vicious beating. Such was the reputation of the man who lived at the top of the hill in Bielefeld, Westphalia, Prussia.

August stared off into the distance, lost in his thoughts. About what? He wasn't really sure. His mind seemed to be drifting from one piece of his life to another. *That is what funerals do to a person, right?*

Bielefeld, 'many fields,' was true to its name. A simple community of a couple dozen or so families who built their barn homes in a loose circle for safety's sake.

Even now, in 1853, it wasn't safe to leave anything in the fields after dark, be it a shotgun, food, or even a farming animal—let alone a human. The night hours were owned by the *Diebe zu Ermorden,* bands of murdering thieves, shielded by the darkness.

> *Oportet enim corruptibile hoc induere incorruptelam et mortale hoc induere inmortalitatem; cum autem mortal...*

August continued watching with no emotion. Actually, his full name was Frederick William August Tüxhorn, he just preferred August. *A man has the right to pick what he wanted to be called. Right?*

He had enough of thinking about the old man. That was a total waste of time. What about his own future? *It was pretty obvious Henry wouldn't be having one.* His humorous internal banter brought another smile to his face. He put his hand up to rub his mustache again so his smile would not be seen.

Henry was the only one who would have stopped him from realizing his dream. The only reason he still lived at home was because his father no longer beat him the way he still did the younger ones, to say nothing of his mother.

August knew his father stopped bothering him at about the age of sixteen, because he had gotten old enough and strong enough to fight back. And fight back he did. Given the chance, August would have killed him, and he was pretty sure Henry knew it, too. Oh, August was on the receiving end of a bad cut over his left eye, leaving a scar for all to see, but at least he was in charge of his own life.

> *...hoc induerit inmortalitatem tunc fiet sermo qui scriptus est absorta est mors in victoria ubi est mors victoria tua ubi est mors stimulus tuus.*

As if a violent temper didn't create enough chaos in their lives, Henry added alcohol to an already dangerous situation. August knew he would never forget the massive mood swings and Henry's dedication to drink which left him unpredictable at best. Extremely dangerous, at worst.

Yes, he was glad the old man was gone. Truth told, August couldn't think of anyone who would miss Henry. He knew the neighbors came to the funeral out of duty and to be assured he was really dead. Violence and drunkenness weren't exactly catalysts for developing friendships. They gave their condolences to the widow, but they didn't mean it. He was pretty sure, Anna knew that, too.

"Frau Tüxhorn, we are so sorry for your loss."

Yeah, right. They weren't one bit sorry. And you can bet Frau Tüxhorn wasn't either. August knew better.

Being honest with himself, he actually felt he should have seen this coming. For the past several years, Henry was getting more and more bizarre. Talking or yelling when no one was around. It was unbelievable the things he had accidentally seen or heard the old man do when he thought he was alone. He was a crazy bugger, that was a fact.

However, no one messed with the old guy. A person may not have liked him, but they didn't want to get on his bad side. August had to give him that. No one screwed with ol' Henry.

Stimulus autem mortis peccatum est virtus vero peccati lex Deo autem gratias qui dedit nobis victoriam per Dominum nostrum Iesum Christum.

The priest made the sign of the cross over the grave, and appeared anxious to leave. August had heard him quietly speak to a neighbor before the service began.

"God has finally done something good for this community. Getting rid of Tüxhorn will make life easier on everyone." The priest was not aware a family member overheard him. Let alone a family member who agreed with him.

August chuckled. He knew what they all were thinking right about now. It was time to get to the best part of these unpleasant occasions - the drinking and eating at the wake.

In the name of the Father, the Son and the Holy Spirit, Amen.

Four of Henry's sons lowered his plain, hastily built wooden casket into the deep hole. August had refused to help his brothers dig their father's grave. He wanted nothing to do with assisting Henry in any way. Maybe it was his way of proving he had the last word. He didn't know for sure, but at least it was over.

August watched as they shovelled the disturbed, cold dirt back into the grave and tamped it down. Graves had to be deep so animals wouldn't find the departed. Not that it would make much difference in this case. *Too late!* August coughed to disguise his sudden chuckle.

Refilling the hole was hard work, and his siblings quickly worked up a sweat in the bitter sunshine. When finished, they left to catch up with the rest of the family, who were headed back home. August trailed along behind, not in any particular hurry to get there.

Henry's time on earth was over. All in all, August felt it had been a good day.

CHAPTER TWO

The procession back to the Tüxhorn house was one of silence. Many felt guilt, due to their feelings of relief at Henry's passing. Others just wondered what kind of wine would be served at Anna's place.

August watched ahead as the entire community crowded into and around the little Tüxhorn *wohlstallhaus,* a small barn with living quarters above, for the occasion's food and drinks.

When he finally arrived, August pushed his way through the crowded house and grabbed his *ledertasch,* which had been packed the night before. He then went down the steps into the little barn below that held the cow, a horse, and a couple of chickens. It was quiet here, and that was what he liked about it.

Opening the large barn door to the sunshine, his mood began to lighten. He had packed his leather pouch, knowing he was ready to move on. He wasn't taking much, but then, he wouldn't need a lot. Nor had he informed anyone of his plans. What business was it of theirs?

Dropping the pouch next to the open door, he stared at it a moment to ponder its contents. He'd packed a change of clothes, certainly; a few personal papers; and, of course, his money. The rest of the space was taken with all the food he could shove in, filling it to capacity.

To avoid the outrageous taxes of the day, Henry hid much of his income in the house. He had for years. It was a box everyone had been forbidden to touch, kept under his and Anna's bed. When he registered his measly income to the government, it raised a few eyebrows, but the way Henry and his family lived, one would have to assume they were poor. Henry had no intention of letting anyone think otherwise.

August had already removed from the box what he felt was his fair share, and it was a lot of money. Inheritance was only shared among the sons. Other than maintenance for the widow, females didn't have any rights to inherit, which was as it should be.

Taking his eyes off the pouch, he looked around. The barn was built into a hill to keep it insulated, and the living quarters just above made it easier to protect what few animals a man could afford to own.

The unusual noise and footsteps above were disturbing to the animals, and they were becoming restless. The horse started stamping his hoof and the cow bawled. Habit made August reach for the pitchfork and start filling up the feed troughs to calm them down. He had to agree with them, though. He didn't like crowds of people either.

He looked down at the pitchfork. How many years had he spent stabbing hay in this place? With the barn underneath the house, there was no getting away from the work that constantly needed to be done.

The endless smell of sweat and excrement from the animals wafting up into the living quarters always made him sick to his stomach. People were just supposed to get used to it, but he never did.

August twirled the tool and watched the three metal spikes spin. Upstairs, his mother, siblings, and neighbors were laughing and drinking vodka and wine. He knew the priest would be the one to consume the most. He always did.

How angry Henry would be if he knew everyone was having a good time at his expense. That thought made August laugh right out loud! Yes, he would be livid that his money was being used to entertain the neighbors, let alone his own family. If he had thought about it at all, it might have stopped him from pulling the trigger.

Did one person care that Henry was dead? Was anyone actually mourning for the old man? August certainly wasn't. But what he did have to do was face his father's suicide.

Incomprehensible? Unimaginable? What described suicide? Only a coward took his own life—then add he did it by blowing his head off. At twenty-two, August just couldn't get his brain around that one. He let the thoughts run through his mind as he stared out the barn door into the hypnotic November sun. What had made him pull the trigger? The answer to that question was beyond him.

The sunshine finally seduced him into stepping outside into the cold, clean air. He could almost smell winter trying to choke the very life out of what little was left of autumn.

Croplands butted up to the little community, but there wasn't anything left to see this time of year.

He gazed down the barren hill at the neighbors' homes running down the slope and back around. The little hamlet was quiet now as they all gathered upstairs.

There wasn't much difference, in the homes that is. All had the small first-floor barns with living quarters above. It would be nice to have some privacy from all of them, but a farmer didn't dare move out onto his own property.

Of course, no one went out to the fields at night, but it wasn't entirely safe during the day, either. There had been daylight attacks from time to time, generally just to take the farmer's lunch food and shotgun. It was hard to believe someone could die over a little bratwurst or a *schrotflinte*.

"God, I really hate this place!" He surprised himself when he realized he had spoken out loud. Not that it mattered in the quiet sunlight. His reference to the Almighty didn't matter either.

August had developed a strong desire to move to the United States of America. He heard barns were separate from their houses, where he wouldn't have to live with their smell. And just look at the *size* of that country! The population there was minimal compared to the unclaimed land. It was ripe for the pickings—his pickings. To live on his land and not be worried about being murdered was a dream come true. That was the way August wanted to live.

He prided himself in being methodical and organized. He kept a list of everything he needed to do, so nothing was over looked. August knew the number one thing on his list today was to immigrate to America. Everything else on his list would be dealt with once he got there.

Now was as good a time as any. Henry could have stopped his leaving, but that threat was gone. It was about to turn 1854, after all. If he didn't go now, when would he get around to it? He wasn't getting any younger. Yes, now was the perfect time.

August was not a big man. Quite the opposite, he stood only five feet six inches tall. But he knew what he lacked in stature, he made up for in looks. He was handsome by anyone's standards, and had learned from a young age to use it to his advantage.

Perfect features, large steel-blue eyes, and sandy hair set it all off to perfection. He could credit his mother for his looks. August thought she must have been pretty when she was young. A strong, stout woman she was, perfect for childbearing. Just the kind of woman a man looked for in a wife. That is, if he wanted a wife and a bunch of kids, which he didn't. Never did. That was not the life for August.

His height, or the lack thereof, was never an obstacle to taking care of himself. August knew he had no problem bringing a taller man physically to his knees by the sheer brute force of his fists, especially when fuelled by his violent temper.

Some felt his father was responsible for the anger in him; others called it the small-man mentality. August knew what they said behind his back, but they were all wrong. First, there was no part of his stupid father in him, and there was nothing wrong with his height. He had proved it time and again.

And he certainly didn't have an anger problem. He just hated stupid people. He couldn't help it if almost *everyone* was stupid. *Boy, August, you are just full of clever thoughts today, aren't you?*

August's share of the old man's money, plus the stash from his own work as a farmer's helper since he was old enough to hire out, would make quite a pot. Okay, add the substantial winnings from some not-so-legal backroom gambling, and he was not worried about his next meal – or any for years to come.

No doubt, good things came to those who waited. But he was not inclined to wait any longer.

Staring up into the blinding noontime sun, his thoughts returned to several months earlier when he met a man in a pub who worked for the shipyards in Bremerhaufen. He had given him a lot of information about emigrating, and even gave him an immigration guide. That was when he made up his mind he was leaving Prussia.

All those months ago, August had worried how he would get around Henry, who would have never wanted his son to have a better life than he had. It looked like Henry solved that problem himself. That would surely make him turn over in his newly filled grave, if he knew.

Stepping back into the darkness of the barn, it took a moment for his eyes to adjust. August knew he deserved better than what he had. And he had decided nothing was going to stop him from getting it.

He had even spent some time trying to learn a little English from a bartender in a pub closer to home. The guy didn't know a lot, but August jumped on what words he could learn. Though not very useful, the man knew a lot of the bad ones, which August learned easily.

One thing he knew for sure, emigrating was number one on his mind. *"Emigrating to get away from the tyranny of the government, and religion..."* Wasn't that what the man in the pub had said?

Prussia was known for its corrupt, Catholic-controlled government. It was just a few years back when Lothar Bucher, leader of the radical democratic party of the Prussian National Assembly, and others with similar views, were sent to prison for encouraging citizens to stop paying taxes to the oppressive government.

August knew they were right, of course. However, most people didn't need much encouraging to hide their money from those crooks. If he stayed here, the government would take most of his inherited money in taxes, leaving him with practically nothing. He wasn't going to let them do it. He was going to take all of his money with him to American, where there were no taxes.

That is, if he could find a way to get around his one little emigration problem. He would have to work on that.

Pitching the last bit of hay to the cow, he let the thoughts of America soak into his very being. Yes, the time was right.

He let out a contented sigh.

~~~

Anna had noticed when August went downstairs. She needed to speak to her son now that the funeral was over. He was the one she always had to keep an eye on. If she didn't, she would eventually be sorry. It didn't surprise her that he was alone in the barn downstairs while family and neighbors were gathered upstairs, eating and drinking. August didn't like people.

As much as she hated leaving her guests, there was something she needed to get done right away. It was the most important thing in her life.

Walking down the stairs into the barn, she found August's back was turned and he seemed deep in thought.

"You should be upstairs," Anna said quietly.

Her voice startled him out of his thoughts. He swung around with the pitchfork pointed at her, apparently ready for battle, if necessary.

"Leave me alone, woman. If I wanted to be upstairs, I would be. You don't tell me what to do." There was no denying the anger on his face.

Anna could see he was his usual hateful self, but she backed away from the pitchfork staring at her. She had to be careful what she said now, and especially how she said it. She was quiet for a few moments.

"Why do you think he did it, son?" The question was quiet but firm. Anna really didn't care what August thought, but she had to know what state of mind he was in before continuing on.

"Why did he do what, *Mutter?* Kill himself? Why did he go into the field to work, but instead put a shotgun under his chin and pull the trigger? How am I supposed to know why that crazy old man did anything?"

August's attitude didn't fool her. She knew he had pondered that same question himself. They all did. No matter the dead man's name, his actions were still a shock.

Of course, there was no explanation for Henry's actions. It was not like he was going to tell anyone, and how could she know the devil's own thoughts? Even after being married to him for twenty-eight years, she was as shocked as anyone. But there was that silver lining, now wasn't there? She was free from the beatings and her children were now safe.

They were safe, except for August. She had to deal with him. Now. Somehow, she had to get him to leave and never come back. There was no way she would continue to live in fear. August was the last straw in a bad pile of hay.

Henry's father was the same. The Lord knew, people wouldn't even mention her father-in-law's name again after he died. No one ever wanted to be reminded of him. Two peas in a pod. No, add August and that made three peas in that evil pod.

Anna knew she had children as sweet as fresh cream, and then there were others who had a time with their tempers now and again, but it didn't last long. Then there was August. He was Henry all over again. Not a redeeming quality in his hard heart, and evil as they came. Did she really give birth to this person in front of her? It didn't seem possible.

As his mother, she knew August could be a charmer. By the time he could talk, he was good at manipulation. By his teens, the evil in his eyes would have been the pride of her father-in-law. She knew even Henry was afraid of him from time to time, though he would have been hard pressed to admit it. But she knew. Anyone with half a brain would have been afraid of August.

The one thing Anna had learned from mean, controlling people such as this, was how to get what she wanted. She simply had to demand the opposite. She was really surprised at how many times it had actually worked over the years. But she only tried it when the outcome was very important, as it was now. She proceeded carefully.

Anna said, "You are the oldest at home. I will need you to work the fields."

"You're kidding, right?" August said quietly with eyebrows raised. She could see him making fists of his hands at his side.

"I am not kidding," Anna stated. But she instinctively backed away from him. She wasn't stupid and knew she was pushing his temper.

"Now that your father's gone, I need help to provide for the young ones." Anna also knew how he hated children.

"He left you plenty of money to live on. I saw what was in that box he thought was so well hidden."

That took Anna back. Glancing over at his leather pouch, she wondered how much of her money August had taken. Yes, it was her money. After all she had been through no one was going to tell her any different. Whatever amount he took, there wasn't anything she could do about it now.

"You have to help out on the farm!" She raised her voice just a little. She flinched when she saw the evil in his cold blue eyes, as August raised his fist to strike. She knew it would probably leave a bruise on her face, but she could tell her strategy was working. She had been in this predicament before, and now she had to do it one more time.

"Du bist verrückt, alte Frau." August growled at her, hatred showing in his eyes, but he lowered his fist.

Anna had no doubts that he did, indeed, believe she was a crazy old woman. She didn't care what he thought of her at this point.

"I am not raising your brats, nor am I staying in this miserable town. I'm leaving for good." August threw the pitchfork, barely missing Anna. Did he want to hit her with it? She wouldn't put it past him.

She watched as he grabbed his leather pouch. He walked out of the barn and, more importantly, he walked out of her life. He never said goodbye, but in her heart, she knew he wouldn't be back. The thought made her smile.

It was time to return to her guests and a good glass of wine. All in all, Anna felt it had been a very good day.

CHAPTER THREE

The only place August felt safe enough to try boarding a ship to America was in the city of Hamburg. It was not the usual hot spot for the upper class to board a ship like Bremerhaufen was, but it also wouldn't have as many government workers checking the validity of emigration papers.

After leaving his mother standing in the barn at Bielefeld, he knew he had a lot of walking to do—about 125 miles. He figured that would take him about five days, depending upon the terrain and the weather. August knew pretty much what he would need, so he felt he had packed enough food. The time was not a problem either, as it would give him a chance to think things through. He definitely had a decision to make.

That chance meeting he was thinking about earlier in the barn came back to mind. It was about six months ago when he stopped into a pub. It was poorly lit, crowded, and smelly. Even though drunks were raising their voices, an old woman's cackling laugh could be heard above everyone else.

August hadn't planned on staying long, only time enough to pull a pint. But, as it turned out, it was long enough. The fellow standing next to him was looking at some papers and August noticed the word "America" on them. Nothing was going to stop him from checking out what the man was reading.

"It's an immigration guide to America. Tons of folks are getting away from all this government and religious tyranny by crossing the pond to America," he said in answer to August's question. The man obviously liked the idea himself.

"I have here some letters from folks in Illinois, America," he went on. "The land is really cheap, only about ten percent of what we have to pay here, and there's a whole lot more of it. They are living big, I tell you. Here, read for yourself." He handed the letters to August.

Even in the dim light, the information in the letters made August's surprised eyes open wide. He couldn't believe some of the things he learned from them. It was in these letters he found out about the separate barns—how big they were and that a man could live alone on his very own land.

"Yeah, I can see you feel the same way I did when I first read them." The shipyard worker chuckled at the look on August's face.

August watched as the man downed the last of his beer and turned to leave. "Wish I could afford to go. I'd do it in a heartbeat, I sure would. You can keep that immigration guide, if you want. I can get another back home."

"Thanks, buddy. I'll sure give it some thought." But August already knew it was *exactly* what he wanted. He clung to the guide like it was his lifeline. Actually, he felt it just might be.

Yes, stopping in that pub had been a life-changing experience. Immigrating to America was now a priority to him. August knew there was just one little hitch. He would not be able to do it *legally*.

The process of emigrating out of Prussia wasn't all that difficult, if you had the right papers. He had to have the proper paperwork signed by the proper people, plus the money for the fare. Only those with money and papers in hand would be the ones to get a visa to leave, the very same visa required to get into America.

Birth or baptismal papers, marriage papers, if appropriate, and a declaration of a person's profession were required. Men also had to show papers of their time served in the Prussian Army, required of all males after reaching the age of nineteen.

Papers August simply didn't have.

He had made a point of avoiding the military these past three years and he wasn't going now. For a thousand years, this part of the world had been in constant turmoil, always on the brink of another war or engaged in one already.

For what reason? August knew the answer to that one. It was always to benefit those in power. He had made up his mind years ago that he was not going to be shot dead for a cause that didn't exist, and one he wouldn't believe in if it did. All, so some pompous government official could open another bottle of vodka tomorrow? He wasn't that stupid.

However, August knew the truth. He needed to have paperwork saying he completed his national duty before he could leave. There had to be something he could do to get around that problem.

His father would have loved this problem. No doubt Henry would have used it to keep his son here. The hatred between them had been so intense Henry would have done anything to ruin the chances of his son ever realizing his dream. Now he was free to leave, if he could just get past this one little problem.

As he walked toward Hamburg, August spent hours going through his options. None of which were legal in themselves, but he wasn't going to lose sleep over having to resort to any one of them. He would do whatever it took.

If he stole someone's papers, there was always the risk of capture when his victim went to the authorities. Prison in Prussia was worse than the military. Not much, he chuckled, but just about.

While mulling over the way to accomplish the theft without getting caught, he stopped walking for the night. It was cold, but he could stay warm in his coat and shield himself from the wind by lying among some trees. He also had to hide himself from midnight thieves. With his pouch for a pillow and his knife easily accessible under it, his thoughts were cut short when he yawned and fell into a shallow sleep, one ear always listening for trouble.

The following day, he ate a cold bratwurst then drank from a creek. He stood by it for a moment, thinking how lucky the old man didn't do himself in a month later. All of the creeks would have been frozen. Just another reason for him to think this trip was meant to be. He then started back on his journey.

August quickly went over his thoughts from the day before. He looked at his list for the ideas that didn't have an X by them.

Another option to eliminate his problem would be to kill someone in possession of all the papers and take on his identity. That would handle the problem of the victim going to authorities to have him arrested.

It would be easy enough to find a man about his age traveling alone, once he arrived at the docks. August knew his good looks wouldn't get him to America, so he needed something fool proof. With further thought, however, he knew taking another identity wouldn't work.

"Well, I can't just steal papers. There's too much risk of getting caught. If I kill the bugger, his identity will be near impossible to match with me, putting me right back where I started." In the middle of nowhere, talking out loud did not concern him. August knew he must make the very best decision possible. His entire future depended upon it.

At his height, it would be hard to find another who had papers stating he looked similar to August. Blue eyes and light hair were uncommon in this area. The odds were miniscule, and even if he found such a person, there was then the added risk of getting stuck with a stupid name like *Unglaublichdumm*. Briskly walking on a barely noticeable farming road, he roared out loud at his own joke. *Welcome to America, Mr. UnbelievablyStupid!* The laughter felt good, even in the cold air.

He had made excellent time during his second day, and by nightfall it felt good to lie down and rest. A tight-knit cluster of trees turned out to be the perfect hiding place for the night. But, only after running off some of the animals who also felt that way. He had a quick bite to eat and his eyes were closed.

During the next few days, August carefully probed each option to see its weaknesses and strengths. As he went down his list of possibilities, he marked them off when they came up with more problems than he wanted to deal with, or ones that were just plain impossible to accomplish.

There was always bribery. He could try to buy his way out of the country. He knew that was possible. The Prussian government was so corrupt; he doubted there were any honest men among them. But August also knew if he came upon the only one that might exist, things would get ugly in a hurry. He would have to prepare for that possibility.

What was the going rate, he wondered? What if he offered too little and insulted the crook? He might pocket the money and turn him in anyway. *Really, August? Crooks can be insulted? Well, anything's possible.*

August was good with numbers and he ran some scenarios through his brain. Wages were miniscule when you worked for the government. That much he knew. So, what if he offered approximately six months' pay? Better yet, a years' pay would certainly get noticed. Bribery was not scratched off his list. Not yet.

None of his options were perfect, but he knew he had to pick one of them. He couldn't let anything stop him. He would be walking into Hamburg the following day. He had to admit, he was pretty excited.

He arrived in Hamburg in the middle of November, marking the end of his trip. First he went about finding a boarding room. Then it was time to check his list.

"Okay, we've come this far… Let's see what we need to do now." Scanning his list, he marked off getting a room.

August had finally decided how he was going to solve his emigration paper problem. It appeared he might have been wrong in his earlier assessment. His looks *would* get him there after all. It was time to use the attributes life had given him to his advantage.

He carried his pouch with him everywhere. There was no way he would let all that money out of his sight. Walking to the docks, he found the ship *Bork Fides* leaving for America in only eight days. He was told this ship normally left from Bremen, but for some reason, it was here in Hamburg. It was a big, beautiful ship that he was certainly not going to complain about.

However, not expecting to leave so soon, August took the time to write out another list of things he needed done, and needed done quickly.

The next few days were busy ones. He shaved off his mustache and checked that off his list. He had been partial to wearing a mustache, because it made him look older and more masculine. He was going to miss it, but August knew he could easily grow it back later.

He bought different clothes, then had his hair cut much shorter. The entire image was coming into play. Most of his list was now accomplished.

There was a small problem with one article of paperwork and he took care of that without too much trouble. And the missing military paperwork would no longer be a problem, because it would no longer be needed.

After crossing the last item off his list, he packed his pouch carefully, leaving out the clothes he would need in the morning, and laid down to, hopefully, spend his last night in Prussia.

The following morning, August carefully dressed in his new clothes. When he looked into the small mirror on the wall, he smiled at the young man staring back.

"Well, would you look at this..." August said aloud to his mirror. With clothes more suited for a teen boy, no mustache, and short hair, he had no doubt he could pass for eighteen. Exactly what he wanted.

His birth certificate was written by a person with very ornate handwriting, as most were. However, not ornate enough for his purposes. After practicing for a while, the night before, he had transformed all of the script, including the numbers, into an almost unreadable floral script.

The end result created a birth certificate that was not easy to read. In this case, his birth year of 1831 was a flurry of script and difficult to tell exactly what the numbers were. A slight bend and the last digit could pass for a five. With a birth year of 1835, he was young enough to leave the country, but not old enough to need military service papers.

When he arrived at the docks, August was once again pleased at the ship he was about to board. It was large, with three massive sails that made it look powerful. Just the sight of it made him excited. Though it really wasn't for him, he could see why some men would make crossing the ocean, their life's work.

He took a deep breath, and boarded with his new ticket. Those gathered on the deck were instructed to take their places below until a ship's officer came to talk to everyone.

Below, there were compartments for each traveller or family. It was smaller below than he would have thought from seeing the outside. The noise level was higher, too. The number of whiny, crying children outnumbered the adults. With his mind on the upcoming scrutiny from a ship's officer, August was not amused with the added irritation.

The ship was finally ready to leave port, and not a minute too soon. August thought he could personally drown every screaming brat on board, before they even set sail, but he had to play the innocent teenage boy without blinking.

One of the officers walked in, and the noise in the crowd came to a standstill as he worked his way through the ship's belly. Even the children seemed to know something very important was happening.

He started checking boarding papers. The crowd was hushed and quietly waited their turn. Anything could go wrong. A box not checked, a faded signature, or a food stain could be reason to deny the holder.

The officer was a tall, slender sort of fellow, middle-aged with a warm smile. Friendly, but not the type you would really pay a lot of attention to. But August was paying him a great deal of attention, as he waited his turn.

The officer filled out the visa for the first two families, and gave a 'welcome aboard' smile as he handed them the coveted paper and moved on. After stepping up to a male passenger, traveling alone like August, the passenger said he couldn't find his emigration papers. Three more ship's officers quickly appeared, seemingly out of nowhere, and physically removed him while he screamed and yelled.

"Someone must have stolen them! I had them with me last night! I need to go on this trip! Please...." Fighting not to be removed from the ship and refusing to go back down the plank, the man finally ended up in the water, with a splash heard by everyone below.

It became even quieter among the passengers. August actually felt as if his thoughts were too loud. The officer continued moving to the next in line as the tied-up ship groaned, seemingly impatient to be set free.

Finally, it was August's turn. The officer looked him in the face and asked for his papers. He noticed the faded name 'Emeric Friedhelm' embroidered on his shirt. August gave him the government envelope that came with the Immigration Guide. He had printed 'August Tüxhorn' on the back of the envelope as instructed.

"August, is it? Are you traveling alone, son?" Friedhelm seemed quite pleasant.

"Yes, sir." August took on the persona of an obedient teenage boy, even raising his voice slightly.

"Why are you leaving us, August?" The man really seemed to take an interest in the good-looking young man with the startling blue eyes, as he went through each of his immigration papers. His confused look at the birth certificate lasted only seconds as he replaced it back in the envelope with a small, impatient shake of his head.

"My cousin already lives there, sir. In Illinois. In America. I am going to go live with him and help him farm. My *Mutter* feels it would be best for me, and of course, she is always right about such things." August was starting to enjoy this.

"Very well." Friedhelm signed the visa with all of the pertinent information and handed it to him with a warm smile. "You enjoy your trip now, August. And you let me know if you are lacking anything, my boy. Okay?"

"Thank you, sir. Yes, sir, I will." August placed the priceless visa in his pouch. It was more precious to him, at that moment, than solid gold. A visa...he had a *visa* to leave Prussia and go to America.

August realized he'd almost stopped breathing, if only for a short time. Struggling not to show any outward signs of relief, he slowly took a few deep breaths and congratulated himself on his brilliant success. He then settled in for the duration of the trip across the ocean.

CHAPTER FOUR

It was the third week in November when the ship finally sailed. After pulling out of port, all the passengers were allowed back on deck. This gave them the ability to watch the land disappear from view. Topside was the place August would spend most of his time for the duration of the trip.

Down below felt claustrophobic to him and he hated all the noise from talking and crying babies. He just couldn't figure out why anyone would want to have kids. He felt it was a waste of a man's resources.

Then there was the constant cooking that went on around the clock. It was enough to drive a man crazy. The constant smells would force anyone up on deck.

Friedhelm checked on him often and treated August like a child who needed protecting.

"What is it with that guy? Why won't he leave me alone?" August found himself not sure whether to appreciate the paternal attention he never received from his own father, or be irritated because he was somehow perceived as being helpless.

Not only did he get special attention from Friedhelm because of his "youth," but he found out the man could speak English quite well! He offered to teach August whenever he didn't have to work. That changed everything. August started looking the older man up when there was a chance for another lesson in English.

It actually surprised him that a lot of English was derived from the German language. Of course, there was the fact that Americans said everything backward, but he would work extra hard at getting the hang of it.

The trip across the ocean would only take a couple of months, but seemed longer to August. He figured the other passengers probably felt the same. It was not something he wanted to do again anytime soon. There was a two-day storm at sea that convinced everyone aboard, including August, they were all goners for sure, but the ship finally settled back into a peaceful rocking motion. During this time, Friedhelm was almost constantly by his side, making sure he didn't make any mistakes that would cause him to fall overboard. August was actually growing fond of him.

Food and fresh water were supplied by the ship for each paying customer, but each family had to do their own cooking. The kitchen area was only about six by twelve feet and wouldn't hold many people at once. Some took to cooking all hours of the night so there wouldn't be any fighting among the women who were trying to feed their families at the same time.

August didn't have to deal with any of that. A few coins given to the right matronly types and they were happy to include him in portions they cooked for their family.

August met his new friend on deck each night as well as during daytime meal breaks. Friedhelm taught him everything he could about the English language, which turned out to be quite a lot. It seemed he had been making this trip for over twenty years. It didn't take long for August to find out what little English he had learned back home wasn't any good at all. He was an eager and excellent student.

"You have a knack for this English, August. Your cousin will be so pleased when you show up already able to speak so much of the language!" August noticed the older man was being the proud father again.

"Thank you, sir. You have been such a blessing to me on this trip. What would I have done without you?" Wide-eyed August gave his biggest and best smile to his friend.

"Think nothing of it, my boy. It's my pleasure to help out." Getting up to leave, he said, "I'll bring you some candy when I come off my shift tonight."

August assumed it must give the man more purpose in life to help whom he thought was a lonely child going off to a strange, new world. One day, August voiced the question that weighed on his mind.

"Herr Friedhelm, you speak so highly of America and you know the language so well; why don't you live there?"

"I plan to someday, son. You see, I'm a widower. My wife and I never had children, but we had each other and life was good. Then she died suddenly and I was left kind of all alone and not knowing what to do with my life. Well, there are still the few family members remaining in Prussia who need my help, so I will be there for them. But when there is no one left to take care of, I'm going to take my last trip over here and stay. It is my dream to die in America."

"I hope you get your dream, sir." August couldn't think of anything else to say. If he could feel affection for another person, it was this man.

Even though food and water was free, alcohol was available for a price. August never even looked at it, since he had to stay firm with his "innocent young man" image, at least for the duration of the trip. It was just as well. One of his shipmates managed to get drunk and fell overboard. No one even tried looking for him. *So much for 'man overboard.'*

Sanitation wasn't the best, but only a few illnesses cropped up. A few actually died and were put overboard, but it was mostly the very old or the very young that were at the highest risk of illness and infections.

Christmas came and went with little fanfare. There were those who felt they needed to sing songs and light candles, but for the most part, it was just another day. It was marked in August's mind because Herr Friedhelm gave him a pen as a present to practice writing his English.

The pen was black, but had a red cap that covered the point to protect it. He was really taken aback, because it was the first Christmas present he had ever been given in his entire life. That was not something you forget. That pen was important to him and he told Friedhelm so. He put it in his shirt pocket with the red cap on top for all to see.

August was aware when it was New Year's Day, happy to have it finally arrive, but the day itself was nothing to celebrate. It meant they were one day closer to their destination.

The clean fresh air on the deck was unlike anything he had ever known and he didn't want to miss any more of it than he had to. He felt free for the first time. He knew this was the highlight of his life so far. He was on a glorious adventure.

America was said to be the same way, where a man could be free. It was almost beyond his imagination, but he clung to that awesome thought.

Then, during the second week in January, 1854, it happened.

"Land *HO*, land *HO!*"

The announcement from the sailor clinging to the mast seemed to be heard no matter what corner of the ship a person was in. August raced to the deck along with everyone else.

"Look, Gerta, look! We made it!"

"Hail Mary, Mother of God! Would you looky there? It's America!"

"Oh, if Poppa could just see this…"

"Momma, pick me up so I can see, too!"

Men, women, and children were jumping up and down, screaming and crying. No one seemed to care that someone might think them foolish or immature. No one did, and for once, August was not even annoyed with them. He felt the excitement himself.

For the first time, he really felt as if he were a young boy. His laughed out loud, a laugh that made it all the way to his eyes. He was on top of the world.

Everyone clung to the railings and the view. The land was still far away, and they could barely see it. Barely, but they could.

Then, as if someone had given a signal, they became silent. There was absolute silence. The only sound heard was the creaking of the ship as it slowly moved forward. It was as if everyone was looking at a ghost. The distant land was really America. August felt it himself. All of a sudden, their dreams and sacrifices had a reason. There it was. America. *It was real!* Even the crew stared at the tiny speck of land ahead.

Slowly, they split up and went about quietly packing up their belongings, getting ready for the landing that would still take another day or so to happen. The closer it came, the more jovial everyone became again. Land! They really *had* made it.

August had to admit he was excited, happy, or just plain giddy. He didn't know which and didn't care. But, at the same time, he would be just as glad to be getting off the boat as everyone else. It was time to stand on something that wouldn't move under his feet. It was a new place to start a new life. He wanted to emigrate, and he did!

"I can't believe this. I made it. I am really here!" August couldn't control the speed with which his mind was working. He had his usual list of things to get done and he was writing like mad, adding more and more of the things that America was going to allow him to accomplish. He would need a second list, right away.

August was not a religious man, but just for a moment, staring at the land in front of him, it seemed as if there was a greater power in charge. Of course, it was just for a moment. No one was in charge except August himself. He knew it and anyone who got in his way would know it, too.

The ship would be doing a turn-around, going back to Prussia one month from docking. Friedhelm had told him they all had to scrub the ship clean and prepare for the return trip. On the last evening aboard, they got together to talk one last time.

"There will only be a few people who will be going back, mostly just to visit relatives. Not too many folks leave America to move to Prussia." Friedhelm grinned widely at his statement. He also seemed happy at the thought of solid ground for a while.

"The ship will be near empty of folks going back," he said, "but it means a whole lot less work for us on the back side."

August knew it was time to close the door on this friendship with the older man. He had to admit, he had enjoyed himself. Friedhelm had been good to him.

"I want to thank you for all you have done for me, Herr Friedhelm. You have made my trip so much more pleasant because you were here." August was saying what he thought an eighteen-year-old boy would say. And he said it in English.

"Nonsense, my boy. It was all my pleasure. I know your cousin will be mighty proud of you." He put his arm around August's shoulders and gave him a squeeze.

August knew he wouldn't be seeing any more of Friedhelm with all the work coming up to prepare the ship for the return trip. He also knew it was time to move on.

The following morning as August was leaving the ship; he stopped on the plank and turned to look for his friend. Finding him, they waved goodbye to each other and August stepped off onto American soil. Yes, he would miss his friend.

CHAPTER FIVE

New Orleans, Louisiana, was amazing. August couldn't think of any other way to describe it. He saw pubs everywhere and people were partying. Immigrants rushed around trying to spend what little they had left from the trip. There was a lot of happy laughter, even if most of it was alcohol induced.

August Tüxhorn was no idiot, however. He knew he was still a very long way from his destination of the State of Illinois. That was where his farm would be. It was more real to him now than ever before. He wasn't about to blow any more money than he had to, in Louisiana.

Most ships went into port around New York State, but coming out of Hamburg, this one slid right into Louisiana in the southern part of the country. He smirked to himself, remembering how he was able to make the trip at all. Illinois turned out to be about the same distance from here than from New York, or so he was told.

"August, ol' boy, you did it!" He laughed out loud, standing in the middle of the street in front of the docks. No one around him even noticed due to their own outbursts of happiness.

After asking some locals for information, he finally found an acceptable boarding house to stay in. It was not one of those expensive hotels downtown. He didn't want to waste money on fancy trimming in a room, when it was just a bed he needed.

He also made a list of other places the local people told him about that he very well might have need of their wares or services.

To August, the incredible thing about these conversations was his ability to do it in English! Oh, he'd stumbled over a couple of words and had no idea what slang was, but he was actually able to understand most of what people said back to him. This revelation was almost as sweet as being here in the first place. He felt mighty proud of himself. English wasn't so hard after all.

He was told about a wagon train going north right through Illinois. That Illinois must be a popular place. He immediately walked to the northwest edge of town and spoke with the wagon master. He was pleased to find out they would be leaving in exactly three weeks from the day he landed, so he signed on for the trip. His timing, once again, seemed perfect.

He marked off 'immigrate to America' from the top of his list, and then 'transportation to Illinois' was scribbled through, but there were other things to get done. He took the time to rearrange his priorities and put his errands in the order they now needed to be taken care of.

Then it was time to deal with a problem he had not anticipated. He should have realized that when he felt like he was on top of the world; the other side would show up – the splitting headaches and the depression. That was how it always seemed to work. First up, then down. He hated these times. On his way back to his room, he picked up a small bottle of whisky. It was the only thing that would stop the problem.

The liquor went down smoothly and the pounding in his head started to let up. He didn't feel quite as bad. He finished the bottle and lay down. His bed was comfortable and he slept soundly on his first night in America.

The following morning, he was up early. The bleak evening was gone, thanks to the liquor. August was relieved. He didn't want to start his time in America feeling awful. This problem had happened about once a year since he was ten or so, but he hoped it had been left behind along with his unhappy past.

When he shaved, he told himself this would be the last time he would remove his mustache. It was time to get his old look back, but he needed one more day. No more haircuts, though. It had been over two months since he had his hair cut, so some length was already back.

That also meant his time wearing these kid clothes would shortly be over. But for today, he still needed to look eighteen.

He also added to his list to pick up some American clothes, a hat, and boots like he had seen on Americans in town. He

MURDER IS A FAMILY AFFAIR

might as well look like he belonged here. His Prussian clothes made him really stand out and he didn't want that.

Now topping his list was to find a bank. He needed to trade all his Prussian money for American dollars. August had already worked the numbers in his head and had a pretty good idea of what amount he could expect.

Mid-January of 1854 wasn't what he had expected. It was cool but comfortable here. Back home, he knew the snow would be deep and keeping warm would be almost a full-time job. New Orleans was definitely a strange place.

He couldn't remember when he had felt so free. Even in this busy town, it wasn't nearly as crowded as Prussia. August almost skipped across the street, weaving around a rider on horseback and a wagon headed toward the mercantile.

The walk to the bank, however, turned out to be a lot happier for August than the time spent inside.

"Another immigrant, huh?" The nameplate on his desk said Peter W. Carson, President. The way he looked August up and down made the hair on the back of his neck stand up. Something was wrong here.

"Yes, sir. I need to convert my money into dollars." August spoke in his kid voice, but formed his words deliberately. He needed this man right now, but wasn't going to be talked down to by anyone. He laid his pile of money on the desk.

August saw that Carson, bank president that he was, just about dropped his jaw when he laid all that money in front of him. He knew he had a whole lot more money than most immigrants. Money bought respect. *Now maybe this weasel will treat me a little better.* What came next was an unwelcome surprise.

44

"Well, the rate is one hundred to one," Peter Carson said.

"That's insane!" August's sudden outburst drew the attention of all the other patrons in the bank. Seeing this, he lowered his voice, bent over the desk, and said, "The sign in the window says fifty to one. In addition, I have been told it has been the same for a month. How can it be double that amount?"

"Well, that was yesterday, kid. Today, it is one hundred to one. Take it or leave it." August watched as the rotund banker leaned forward in his squeaky chair, at least as far as his huge belly would allow, and looked him straight in the eye. He wanted to grab him by the throat there and then.

August knew the banker was robbing him blind. Why? Was it because he was an immigrant, or because he was thought to be a stupid kid? Maybe both, but at this moment, the fat man had the upper hand. Carson owned the only bank for miles around that would convert foreign money into American. August had already learned that much.

In his head, August quickly figured up what he would lose. He stood as tall as he could, slowly looking around the bank deep in thought, then back to Carson.

"Okay." That was all August said. Now was not the time to deal with this thief.

Carson chuckled and picked up August's money. Rising from his chair, he walked toward the back of the bank and out of sight. He came back a couple of minutes later with the American dollars and threw them on his desk.

August looked at the pile of crisp new dollars, banded neatly together. There were not nearly as many bundles as there should have been.

Carson put a piece of paper in front of him that he was to sign acknowledging he had received his money. The man held out a pen for him to use, but August ignored him and grabbed his own pen from his shirt pocket, pulled the red top off, and then used the fat man's ink to sign his name.

Very carefully, he capped his pen and put it back in his pocket with the red end up. He picked his money up and put it into his bag. Without a word, he turned and walked away.

Mr. Carson didn't know him very well. August had no doubt that, given more time, the banker would get to know him a whole lot better.

In three weeks he would be on his way with the wagon train. Others, also waiting to leave but couldn't afford the extravagance of a boarding house, pitched a tent or lived out of their covered wagon at the edge of town and cooked over an open fire. August was glad he could afford more comfort for himself.

He marked off 'exchange money at bank' and saw the next item was to get registered at the Immigration Office. *Yes, let's get that done.* He had a visa—a legal, proper visa.

The Immigration Office was busy, since the *Bork Fides* had come into port. August stood in line for almost an hour before he was called into the government office in New Orleans. He was livid about the wait, but had to hide his feeling from the government clerk taking names. He didn't need any trouble after getting this far.

"Spell your surname, please." A scrawny guy with round glasses grabbed a new form and waited on him. He spoke perfect German, so August figured him for an immigrant himself.

"T-Ü-X-H-O-R-N." *Get it right*, August thought.

"Do you want to add an e?" the clerk said in German.

"What?" August had no idea what he was talking about.

"The English language does not have an umlaut. Most people just add an e after the umlauted vowel so it will sound about the same in English. Do you want me to spell your name as T-U-E-X-H-O-R-N?"

"No." August thought that sounded stupid. "No added letters."

"Very well. The umlaut will be removed. What's your destination, sir?" The glasses kept sliding down his thin nose, causing him to keep pushing them up. It was a lot more irritating to August than it seemed to be to the clerk.

Gritting his teeth but showing his nicest smile, August said in English, "I will be going to Illinois to start a farm, sir."

Surprised to hear a new immigrant speak the language, let alone doing it fairly well, the clerk smiled. Then he looked back at August's visa.

"A little young to own your own farm, are you not?" The clerk's curiosity was piqued, but he smiled.

Fighting for an acceptable answer, he smiled and said, "Yes, I suppose I am. I do have two cousins that are already here who said they would live with me and help me with the farm."

"Very well. How much land did you want to buy? It will be five dollars an acre, only in multiples of five."

Five dollars. Okay. "I believe eighty acres would be a reasonable start. Don't you?" August grinned, knowing most of his fellow shipmates could not spend that kind of money after the cost of getting their families across the ocean.

The immigration officer's eyes glanced up and his glasses slid down. He raised his eyebrows and smiled. "Well, I think eighty acres would be a perfect place to start, sir."

See. Money got respect and August had money. Not all of his money yet, but that would come.

August's mind went back to thoughts of having half his money stolen by that crooked banker. He was reliving every second of his time in that bank, when he heard, "Uh, *Herr Tüxhorn*...sir?"

August brought his mind back to the clerk.

"We show such a place for sale just outside of Salisbury, in LaSalle County, Illinois."

August told him that sounded just fine to him and the deal was made.

Four crisp, new American hundred-dollar bills changed hands. The clerk finished neatly writing the answers on the form. He then handed August his immigration papers and the deed to his property. August was told to register that deed at the county seat as soon as he arrived.

Then, in English, the clerk said, "Mr. Tuxhorn, welcome to America."

August smiled and nodded his head before turning to leave. The looks of respect were on the faces of everyone in line behind him that had understood the transaction. August figured after making a success of those acres, more could always be obtained. At least, that was the plan.

Eighty acres almost guaranteed a farm would succeed. The news quickly spread among the immigrants. Mr. Tuxhorn was the man to know. He took out a piece of paper and marked off 'register at immigration' and 'buying a farm' from his to do list. He reviewed the rest of the things he had to accomplish before the wagon train left. Then he added 'Peter Carson' to the bottom of that list.

Over the next week, he went about taking care of the rest of his business. The long list kept him busy. There were the American clothes and boots to buy. Check. Obtain a fine horse for the trip. Check. Pay for the livery to take care of the horse until he left. Check. Purchase saddle and saddlebags. Check. Throw away all Prussian clothes and footwear. Check. Buy revolver and holster. Check.

August had no problem getting these things taken care of, but something was starting to bother him. As he took care of all these errands, he kept feeling as though he was being followed. A figure kept moving about in his peripheral vision, mostly outside when he was on the street.

Maybe it was his imagination, but when he walked out of the livery, he could have sworn someone ducked down an alley out of eyesight. Then, just yesterday when he left the mercantile, someone seemed to be watching him out a window from across the street. As soon as he looked up, the curtains were closed so he couldn't see in.

Why was he imagining crap like this here in America? It was in Prussia you couldn't trust anyone you knew, let alone a stranger. But still...

Since the majority of his errands were now taken care of, he found he had less than two weeks remaining before his departure. A couple of times he had purchased a bottle of liquor and taken it to his room, but one night, he decided he wanted some company and there was a cute blonde in the pub, er...*saloon*, who suited his fancy just fine.

With his hair growing out and his mustache coming back, he felt more like himself with every day that passed. That, and his American clothes gave him an older, more distinguished look. He was certainly as manly as anyone else in the saloon.

The cute blond had no problem sitting on his lap and intimately teasing him. When he finally got around to the question of price, a deal was struck. He bought another bottle and they headed to the boarding house.

As he walked out of the saloon with his arm around the blond, he saw a man run across the dark street and out of sight. Was that man running away from him? Or was he running for another reason? Well, it wasn't going to ruin the evening he had planned.

Once in his room, the blonde said her name was Sarah Brown. They drank and teased until he told her to get undressed. Their time in bed went quickly and he rolled over with a satisfied grin. August didn't realize it, but he dozed for just a moment. When he was startled awake, what he saw filled him with rage.

Sarah had quietly gotten dressed. She had apparently decided the agreed-upon price was not enough. She started rummaging through his pouch to find more, when she came upon his large stash of money. She let out a gasp at the sight of it, and that was what woke him.

As her hand reached for it, August slipped out of bed and had his arm around her waist and his knife against her throat, before she even touched the money. She tried to scream, but couldn't. Rage filled him to the point of murder. How easy it would be to slice her pretty little neck wide open.

Slicing the throat of a thieving whore would not give the law a second thought. Or would it? He wasn't all that sure about what American law said. He knew back home, he could have killed her and thrown the body away, but he didn't want to chance it here.

August opened the door to his room and physically threw her out. She almost went over the second story bannister, but managed to keep from falling.

He stepped out of his door, grabbed her by the hair, and jerked her back toward him. With her back pressed against him, he whispered quietly into her ear.

"Don't you ever come near me again or tell anyone about my money. Do you hear? If you do, I will kill you with my bare hands." August's voice was low and cruel, with no sign of his earlier passion. She not only heard him, she believed him. She ran down the stairs and out into the night, never once looking back.

After returning to his room, he was furious with himself.

"How could you, you idiot?" He scolded himself as he paced the floor for an hour. He punched his fists at invisible targets and kicked his feet at nothing. "You should have *known* that street trash would try to rob you. Awww!" He wanted to pull his hair out; he was absolutely livid.

August spent that night, and every night after, with a chair braced under the door handle and his pouch under his head. His new revolver lay on the table by the bed within easy reach, as well as his knife. He was so upset with himself for even letting her into his room.

Things didn't get any better by the end of the week. Two nights later, he encountered yet another problem. Feeling closed up in his room, he decided to go for a walk after dark when everything died down. Going out the back way, he saw a man hiding in the same back alley. His back was to August, and he was looking around the corner toward the street.

It was him. It had to be him. It was the guy who had been following him, lurking around corners, and running through the darkness. But this time, August recognized him, even from behind. He quietly walked up behind the man until he was close enough to touch him - and then he tapped him on the shoulder.

The man jumped a foot and turned to look in the face of August Tuxhorn. At first, August was amused. He gave a big smile, and said hello.

"Why, *Herr Friedhelm,* how are you? What on earth are you doing off the ship, let alone in this back alley? What are you...?" He stopped before he could finish his sentence. The look in Friedhelm's eyes told him something was wrong. Very wrong.

The man stayed quiet for a moment and then the look on his face changed from fear to intense anger.

"You lied to me. You are not an eighteen-year-old boy. Look at you! I have been watching and you are no child. You are old enough to use the services of a trollop. I saw you myself. You lied to get your visa."

Oh boy. August didn't need this complication now. *Friedhelm, please just go away.* But he didn't. His anger had him on a roll.

"The only reason age would have mattered for a visa is if you didn't serve in the military. That it, Tuxhorn? You were too much of a coward to fight for your country?" Friedhelm was obviously livid at having been so deceived.

"Now how do you know who was with that girl?" August was trying to put some doubt in Friedhelm's mind.

"How did I know it was you? Of course it was you, an *older* you. And...look, your pen! I could see the red cap in your pocket, too!" He was fit to be tied.

August glanced down at the red cap extending out of his pocket. How proud he had been to show it off. He remained quiet and gave the man a small smile and shook his head. *Why does he want to cause me trouble now? Why? I just want to get on with...*

"You are in a lot of trouble, *Herr Tüxhorn.* I will have you deported back to Prussia immediately! It will be easy to prove you lied on your application for the visa. You will have to travel back with me, and I can assure you, I won't be your caring friend this time!" August could see Friedhelm anger grew, as the realization of how he had been taken, was soaking in.

Now see? August was thinking. *He used my old name. Why did he go and do that? He's gonna tell and I will not be an American citizen after all. I can't risk that. No, I just can't risk that, now can I? This is entirely his fault. He has left me no choice...*

Friedhelm didn't even see him move. In less than a second, August grabbed the man around his neck and snapped it. The older man was dead before fear could even register in his eyes.

August picked him up and carried him along the alley to the back side of the saloon. There was a dark stairway that men used when leaving the building, after finishing with one of the loose women upstairs. He laid him face down right at the bottom of the stairs, pulling one leg up to the second step. For all intents and purposes, it looked like Friedhelm was coming down the stairs, maybe had too much to drink, fell, and broke his neck.

August muttered, "Sorry, old friend," as he walked away. Fatigue finally overcame him and he knew there was still enough time to catch a few hours of sleep. Behind the boarding house, he threw away his Christmas present pen.

August read about Friedhelm in the paper the next day. It wasn't major news, just a mention that he was found. The paper said it was obviously an accidental death. August even heard some men tease each other about not getting too drunk before going down those back stairs.

August figured the sheriff wouldn't even get involved. Even if all of the women working that night denied he was there, their soiled reputations would insinuate they took on so many men they couldn't remember them all. Too bad about Friedhelm, though. He really was a nice man.

August knew he had been of some help to his old friend, though. He had granted the man his wish to die in America.

CHAPTER SIX

The boarding house worked out. However, what originally seemed a happy place had turned to disgust for August. After the first two weeks of dealing with the seedier side of life, he lost any taste for the town.

New Orleans was nothing more than a den of thieves and whorehouses. Loose women were trying to get a man's life savings after getting him drunk. Men were preying upon the immigrants by "selling" promises that didn't exist, or, like the banker, just out and out stealing a man's money.

August was no genius, but he sure wasn't that stupid. He'd seen men in the saloons drop over unconscious after a barmaid gave him a drink. The man would then be drug off to a back room, only to be thrown out the back door. August knew he would wake up the next morning without a dime on him. If the victim made any accusations, he might just disappear altogether. Immigrants were a dime a dozen and one would not be missed.

When August chose to drink, he bought an unopened bottle and sat at a table against the wall, or took it back to his room alone. Either way, he always did his own pouring. Nobody was going to slip him anything to knock him out. These people were just thieves.

Time in New Orleans was boring when a man didn't live the party lifestyle. He spent a lot of time at the edge of town practicing with his new revolver. He also learned how to saddle his horse and even had a chance to ride a little, but to August, the three-week wait seemed forever. The good news was, now there was only a week remaining before he left with the wagon train.

He liked to spend time talking to the men down at the inn where the stagecoach from Texas came in. A couple of them had even been to Illinois and told August everything they knew about the place.

One of the things that emotionally drew him was the four seasons. He was used to that and didn't want to swelter in year-round, humid heat. Illinois would be a good place to live.

But it was more than learning about his new home; he was practicing his English more each day. Some phrases came harder than others, but he was doing pretty well. He didn't want to be around people he couldn't understand. How would he know if they were up to no good?

August soon heard the townsfolk were horrified when a prostitute by the name of Sarah Brown ended up dead about six days before the wagon train was to leave. Her body was found outside of town, lying under a tree.

He read in the paper that she was choked to death. He also read that next to her body was a dollar bill. It was perfect, like it had just been minted, or maybe it was a new bill from the town's bank. It had never even been folded. Crisp and clean, it was.

He also heard someone say the sheriff was going to need some time to put the pieces together, but it seemed the townfolk wanted fast answers he didn't have.

August knew he could help the sheriff with his problem, but to do so, he would need a few more days.

~~~

The sheriff was mighty puzzled over Sarah's death. Who would want to kill a pretty girl like that? Where was he going to find the time to figure it all out? He just didn't know what to make of it. Until now.

It was the day before the wagon train was leaving, and he had a hornet's nest on his hands. Old Pete Carson was found dead, too. The owner of the bank himself was found dead about half a mile from town.

It seemed he went into his own bank in the middle of the night, opened the safe, and withdrew a very large sum of cash. He wrote a note saying he was leaving and was sorry about killing Sarah. It was his handwriting, all right. Old Carson had been around for almost twenty years, and the sheriff himself knew what his chicken scratching looked like. Within hours, the town was buzzing like irritated bees.

The sheriff figured he must have been galloping away really fast, because he died from a hard blow to the front of his head. His skull was crushed right across his forehead. The splinters were still in his head to prove it. There was a low hanging tree limb almost above him, so it was obvious he didn't see it coming and rode headfirst right into it. It was bad enough to give a person a headache just thinking about it, and the sheriff knew it was the talk of the whole town.

Now he had to set it all straight for the townfolk. They deserved the truth and it was his job to give it to them. So he put his hat on and stepped out of his office. It wouldn't do any good to put it off any longer.

"Hey, Sheriff!" "Sheriff, what have you heard?" "Sheriff, is it true?" "Have we got a killer on the lose?" "Sheriff…what…?" The group of people standing around was growing by the minute.

"Okay," the sheriff said, standing on the porch in front of his office. It was a refreshing, clear, sunshiny day, the kind that made a person remember why he liked living near the water so much. He was surrounded by a bunch of people looking for some kind of closure and there was no need trying to ignore them.

"Okay, settle down, folks. Here's what happened. One Mr. Peter Carson hired the services of one Miss Sarah Brown. For a reason we will probably never know, something got out of hand and he killed said Miss Sarah Brown." The sheriff was feeling pretty good about having solved this so soon. That was why he was the sheriff and they weren't. He had crime solving *talent*.

"Mr. Peter Carson had a bad week of guilt over what he had done to Miss Sarah Brown, so he decided to leave this town before he got caught. I'd already had my suspicions about him." The sheriff just added that last bit to make himself look good. Fat old Carson was the last person he would have suspected in the killing of a working girl. What working girl would ever want to take him on, anyway?

"Mr. Peter Carson opened the bank vault," the sheriff went on, "and took a substantial amount of money out of it. Riding fast away from here, he was hit by a low tree branch that knocked him off his horse and killed him dead. His horse was nearby and some money was strung all over the area. Most likely, the biggest part of the money was blown away by last night's wind and is now at the bottom of the bay. Now that's the way it was. Go home and leave me to my job."

"Nice work, Sheriff," someone called out. "Yeah!" "Thanks, Sheriff," called others.

He grinned at the crowd, tipped his hat and walked back into his office, as they started to disperse. This case alone should have been enough to get him elected again next year. He put his boots up on the desk and opened a new bottle of whiskey. He really needed a drink after all this calamity.

Fighting, robbery, dead bodies, and such—it had sure been a busy month. It generally was when a new ship came into port. Not this many *bodies,* to be sure, but plenty of drinking and fighting. It was a really good thing he had it solved so quickly.

Sure, old Carson helped solve the puzzle by writing the note and running with the money, but the putting of two and two together was his job and he got it done. That he'd taken all that money didn't surprise the sheriff either. That old buzzard was a thief and most everyone knew it. Not only immigrants, but his own townfolk had suffered financial losses at the man's hands. It served him right. Luckily, he had never had need of Carson's services. He kept his money in a jar at home. Now he was glad he did.

The sheriff took a long gulp from the bottle. He was feeling good and decided he might just head over to the saloon and see which one of his favorite girls was working tonight. Too bad about Sarah, though. Even if she *had* stolen his pocket watch that night all those months ago…

~~~

Three weeks to the day from the boat landing, the wagon train was lined up and ready to leave. August was mighty glad to be leaving with it. A good horse, some food, and a fortune in American money in his saddlebags were just a preview of the new world he would have.

While waiting for the signal to move out, he remembered one more thing he had to do. He reached into his shirt pocket and brought out his to do list and a pencil. He marked Sarah Brown and Pete Carson off. With a smile, he figured *now* he was ready to go.

Goodbye Babylon; hello Illinois.

~~~

Once on the move, he quickly realized he liked his new mare. He had gone all out and bought the best, even though she was almost twice the price of the average ride. For a horse, August figured it always paid off in the end if you got a good strong one.

Oh, he had ridden her a time or two in the past couple of weeks, but not very far. Where was he going to go? Ride from one end of town to the other? One thing he did spend time doing was to learn how to saddle his horse and how his new equipment worked. All that time at the livery was how he found out so much information about what was going on in town, as well as across the country.

Riding mostly behind the wagon train, he stayed to himself. For about the first week, he was mighty uncomfortable at the end of the day. Riding a horse took some getting used to! For the first couple of nights, he needed a bottle to take the edge off the pain he felt between his legs. A time or two, he came close to tears over it.

Men in America lived on these creatures, so he knew he had to plug on. Back home, a horse was for pulling a plow. Only the rich could afford one just for riding around on, but, then again, he was rich now. He had to get used to it.

They first headed north to Jackson, Mississippi, where a couple of the wagons stayed. A day later, they headed on up to Memphis, Tennessee. August loved being out in the fresh air. The weather was nice and they didn't run into much rain, which he had been told was to be expected in February.

By the time they got up north to St. Louis, over half of the wagon train had left them, their destinations having been reached. August had finally gotten over most of the pain of riding in the saddle all day.

One problem came up about then. They rode right into a lot of snow. It was making it harder to drag the wagons through it, even on the well-worn trails.

Patience not being a virtue, August became irritated whenever a wagon broke down and everyone had to stop. *Enough, already.* He almost decided to leave them behind, but he didn't know the rest of the way to Salisbury, Illinois, so he waited. He gritted his teeth and waited. Truth of it was, even on horseback it was slower going in this weather, however, he needed someone to blame for his impatience.

After leaving almost everyone in St. Louis, the wagon train consisted of only three wagons and two on horseback, August being one. They rode straight north into LaSalle County. The town of LaSalle was the actual county seat and just as beautiful as they said it would be.

February in Illinois was a glorious sight for August. Clean, fresh air and snow let you see for miles. It was a decent-sized town and one that suited him fine. It was a far cry from that den of sin, New Orleans.

Rounding up a boarding room for the night, he then went to file his deed with the county clerk. That was first thing on his new list. At the courthouse, he had no problems getting his paperwork filed and he was given a map to the land he owned, not far from where he was now, near the town of Salisbury.

"Here you go, Mr. Tuxhorn. Just follow that map and you can't miss it. When you leaving?" The county clerk was a tall thin man, not much older than himself.

"I will be leaving in the morning, if I get everything taken care of today." August was anxious to finish the traveling and settle down on his land. Lord, just to *see* it would be a dream come true!

"Mighty fine." The clerk said. Then he added with a smile, "You had better hurry, though, if you want to see Salisbury."

He found a dozen men standing around the livery who were looking for work. A deal was struck and six of them agreed to leave with August in the morning. He then bought a couple of large wagons, which he loaded up with a lot of the supplies, blankets, and tools he would need to get started. Of course, he had to buy the horses to pull those wagons. He didn't mind that. They would come in handy once there.

One large purchase was a wood stove. He then bought a bunch of already cut timber. A big extravagance, that timber, but he would need it this time of year to build a shelter from the weather. The only other solution was to stay in town until the weather cleared up in the spring, but August was not waiting that long to get on his own place.

The new hands would be the ones to actually drive the wagons out to his land. Everything had been marked off his to do list and he could now get a good night's sleep. As soon as he arrived at his land, he would need to make another to do list. He expected that one to be quite long.

In bed that night, he thought about the odd statement the county clerk made. *What did he mean by 'you'd better hurry?'* Were they going to move the town or something? August spent some time trying to figure out the puzzle, but finally let it go in favor of sleep.

CHAPTER SEVEN

The following morning, August was rested and ready to start for Salisbury. His new farmhands rode along with him. It was only a couple hours ride, but a little slower going with the wagons. However, they managed to arrive by noon.

One of the first thoughts he had as he rode into town was, *Guess the clerk was wrong, seems the town was still here after all.* He almost laughed out loud at his observation.

August wasn't interested in checking out the small town. After all this time, he wanted to see his land. He had gone through a lot to get here. He rode on through, followed by his crew and wagons to his new farmstead. Upon arriving, he was very pleased with what he saw.

As far as he could see were rolling hills with tall trees. Even barren, the trees provided a homey feeling that August immediately felt. The new farmhands even commented on how nice it would be to live here. Parking the wagons in the shelter of some trees, they spent the first few days surveying every foot of the eighty acres to find the best place to build the house and barn. There was a lake the size of about nine acres. It would be perfect for the livestock he was going to buy.

With the lumber he purchased in LaSalle, they quickly built a one-room structure where all of them could sleep. The wood stove was put in place and they had heat when they needed it at night.

With the snow season in full force, all they would be able to accomplish was to pound the stakes into the ground to mark the future building sites. August still found it thrilling. His house and barn. His farm. His life.

One weekend in early March, a snowstorm came in that kept them in their little shelter for three days. As nothing else could, the whole bunch of them were ready to do any kind of work to get out of that room.

He counted a bit on one of his hired hands, who was born in America and knew about building barns. The guy drew a decent picture for him. He couldn't believe how big it would be. He made the guy ride with him over to a neighbor's place just so he could see for himself. *Yeah, they are huge, all right!* American barns would be one thing that would amaze August for most of his life.

Riding on his own land was like being on top of the world to him. The quiet was so overwhelming, he could actually feel it. He had never known anything like it. Living in Prussia, sailing on the ship, and then joining the wagon train had forced him to live with the constant noise of other people his entire life. Not anymore. The intense quiet of his own land was like sweet music to his ears. Coming to America had been the right thing to do, no matter *what* it took.

Even though major building would have to wait until spring thaw, they started putting up fences. That would take the better part of two months working seven days a week in the cold weather. It wasn't easy, but it had to be done. The fencing kept him running back to LaSalle for more and more wire. It amazed him how much it was taking to surround eighty acres.

Next were the pens around the barn for livestock. It was the end of April when it was all done and the winter weather had retreated.

One of his farmhands came up with the list he now needed.

"So, you say we should have fifty cows, a couple of bulls, ten horses, and some chickens? I can round them up in LaSalle my next trip. Some of you boys will have to go with me." August was pleased with their progress thus far.

During the months of May and June, livestock was purchased and it was time to start on the buildings. His house and barn had to be finished by the fall so he would be in his own home before cold weather set in.

It was time for more supplies, so he left his hands cutting down trees and he took a wagon into Salisbury. As soon as he reached the edge of town, he saw they had put up a new sign. The name of the town had changed from Salisbury to Peru.

"Well, I'll be. That clerk in LaSalle did know what he was talking about. Salisbury really *is* gone." August chuckled, thinking about what the clerk had said all those months ago. Okay, Peru it was. It felt right. His whole life was new, and now even the town's name was, too.

Peru was not as big as LaSalle—just a small stop in the road, really. There were not many people here. They had a post office, a store, and Horton's Pub, owned by an old Englishman named George Horton.

He purchased some of his needed supplies, but knew he would have to go back to LaSalle for some of the higher quality needs.

The spring and summer of 1854, came to Illinois, and August had his hands full. The house and barn were started, but he knew he had a deadline to get them both completed. He had been told it would most likely be snowing in October, but it had been known to start in September.

One problem that bugged him all summer was the need for more help. It was amazing how many guys would just walk off the job and quit. They always blamed him, and it made him madder than a snake. He would ride into LaSalle, hire more folks, and by the time he got back, some other lazy bum would have gathered up his things and left.

They were no-good buzzards. He wouldn't take their lip or their sloppy work. This was his place and his money. He would tell them what to do and how to do it.

He was not going to concern himself with crops this year. He could afford to wait until the following spring. That gave him and his hands plenty of time for building structures. That was, if he could keep enough hands to *do* the building.

"Boss, what about the bunkhouse?" One of his hands stepped up as he was looking at the beginnings of a nice barn.

Before he could even ask, the hand knew it would need explaining.

"That's the place for the hands to sleep. Beds on top of each other are called bunk beds here. We'd bunk down on those beds, so we call it a bunkhouse. Normally they can handle about six or eight men, but you have eight working for you already." He grinned.

"Let's make it to sleep fifteen." August was thinking outloud.

"Fifteen? Boss, that seems a bit…" He backed off when he saw the warning look in August's eyes.

"There will be a time when fifteen will not be room enough. Now make it happen."

August always got disgusted with narrow-minded people. You had to think about tomorrow. But that was why he was the boss and they weren't. They best never forget it. Sure, he didn't need that many men now, but he planned to buy out any land that came available that touched his. He was planning for the future, and a bright one, at that.

It took until the end of September to complete the house and barn. Luckily, the weather held out quite nicely. In fact, it was reported to be one of the finest Indian summers that part of Illinois had seen in some time. August was grateful for the timing.

He went into LaSalle on many occasions, picking up furniture and beds for his home and the bunkhouse, as they arrived by train. Most of that stuff had to be ordered, because it wasn't available locally. The stove was removed from the one-room shelter and put into the bunkhouse. The shelter was then turned into a chicken coop.

Cattle were kept in the pens and the horses had brand-new stalls in the barn. Chickens clucked and laid eggs. Even a couple of stray dogs were hanging around. It was beginning to feel like home.

On October 1, 1854, August moved into his new two-story home with a wide front porch that went around three sides of the house. He couldn't believe it. He felt like a king. Just one floor of his house was the size of the house and barn put together back in Prussia. And then he had a top floor just for bedrooms.

The barn, of course, was three times the size of his house. He couldn't figure that one out. He could keep as many horses as he wanted. Some days, he just couldn't take it all in. Life was good.

That fall, he decided to plant winter wheat. It didn't take more than a couple of weeks. Once that was done, there wasn't much more to worry about through the winter. Or so he thought.

"Boss, Boss!" A farmhand was galloping up to the house.

August stepped outside onto the porch. "What the devil are you yelling about?"

"Injuns, Boss. Injuns done killed the Bakers west of here!" The man looked like he was going to have a heart attack.

"What Indians?" August was not taking this in. Indians? Why would Indians be in these parts?

He called all the hands together and had six of them circle the house and barn with rifles. The other two would ride into Peru, with him, and see if they could find out what was going on.

Upon making it to Peru, he noticed a crowd at Horton's Pub. Stopping there, he managed to push his way in.

"I'm telling ya, we're all gonna die!" one man cried out.

"Take it easy," the sheriff said. "No need to get riled until we find out where they went."

"What happened, Sheriff?" This time it was August. "I just got into town."

The sheriff turned around to face him. August could see he looked exhausted.

"We ain't had no Injun trouble here for some time, but seems three renegades raided Baker's farm and killed all seven of them, even the children. Baker managed to kill one of them, before he got it. I hear it ain't a pretty sight out there. Injuns have a way of butchering the remains of their victims."

The sheriff continued, now talking to everyone. "There is nothing you can do standing around here. Go back to your farms and guard them. Be prepared. Have someone with a rifle awake at all times. Now get out of here."

August turned to leave, but noticed a pretty lady looking back at him. She had light skin and dark hair. Thoughts of her were fleeting, however, as he tried to get this idea of Indians wrapped around his brain.

He was almost in a state of shock all the way home. Even the hands were totally silent. Indians? It was supposed to be safe here. No midnight raiders or anything. Well, he wasn't going to let anyone take what was his.

Half the men stood watch for twelve hours and then the other half took over. It was a ritual that went on for a week. Then word came that the last two renegades had been killed down south. But August was having none of it. It was another week before he put his men back on their regular schedules.

After the scare, things slowly returned to normal, even to the point of August leaving the farm. He was riding over to LaSalle for supplies most of the time. The selection was greater, even though the ride was a couple of hours farther.

It was during the first week in November that he felt it coming on. The pounding headaches, the sadness. After a week, it didn't seem to want to go away, so August was forced to turn to the bottle. He stayed drunk for two days.

It would have been an uneventful episode had it not been for that farmhand who mouthed off to him one morning. Rage at the idiot's insolence caused him to beat the man pretty bad. He was carried off the property by other hands and taken to Peru for a doctor. The man had few teeth left, a broken arm, and no pride remaining.

August felt it served the hand right, and he felt a whole lot better. His head stopped hurting and his mood picked up.

CHAPTER EIGHT

Peru, Illinois, had a lot of decent German folks living there. There were more German immigrants than people from any other country, actually. Seems he was always running into someone speaking German. He, however, preferred his new language, and kept from falling back into what might be easiest.

He managed to keep the farmhands somewhat busy through the winter by riding the fence line, making sure everything was perfect, and taking care of the livestock. August, himself, would ride into LaSalle from time to time and stay a couple of days. He would check out livestock, tools, clothes, and, of course, the ladies. The year ended and 1855 began. He had accomplished a lot in the year he had been in America.

There was a saloon in LaSalle that he would frequent. A little lady named Denise always caught his eye. She was young, appearing to be no more than nineteen. She had long dark hair that flowed freely over her shoulders and a teasing smile.

He felt comfortable with her, and had been using her services for several months now.

August figured she was just a simple, uneducated girl trying to make a living. The one thing he noticed about her, though, was her sad chocolate brown eyes. His interest wasn't in her beauty, because she really didn't fall into that category. There was a pain that went way into her somewhere that no one could touch, and it showed in her face, making her the type men wanted to protect. He figured she got a lot of business because of it.

He would let her spend the whole night with him in his room. That was something he had never allowed before, but she was different. He felt he could trust her. Besides, he didn't carry more money than he needed on any particular trip anyway. It was not like his entire fortune was laying out for all to see. That incident in New Orleans was never far from his thoughts.

It was one night in late January, 1855. August had finished adding wood in the stove to keep the room warm. They were snuggled under the covers when August learned where the sadness came from.

"Why is it you never married, August?" Denise asked him when he had returned to the bed. Her voice could only be described as tiny.

"I don't know, girl. I just never thought about it. Why would I want to take on the responsibility of someone else when I don't have to?" For once, August was being as honest as he could.

"Sounds like you've never been in love," she said sadly. She sat up with her legs crossed next to his reclining body.

"Ha! Is there such a thing? Come on, it's a fantasy. Only stupid people believe in such a thing. Marriage is for idiots." He didn't understand what people found so intriguing about that word.

"Yes, there is. I was in love once. My Ben was the most wonderful man in the world. Everything about him was perfect. His smile, twinkling eyes, sexy voice…"

"Well, then, why aren't you enjoying his advances instead of being here with me?" August smirked, not really wanting to hear about her other lovers.

"He got killed by Injuns." Her voice cracked. Now she had his attention.

"What Indians?" August sat upright. He wasn't sure he heard her right.

"It was two years ago. It was over by Fort Dearborn. My husband, Ben, was part of the patrol trying to save the fort. Injuns killed most all of them. My Ben included." Her voice was low and introspective. August thought she was going to cry.

"Well, Denise, look at it this way. Him being dead, he isn't here to see you being a whore and all…" He chuckled at his own joke. It wasn't his fault she was a widow and he sure didn't want that putting a damper on her performance tonight, so he poured them another drink and got down to business.

The next day, he left LaSalle. Winter had settled in and he didn't get back as soon as he thought he would. Actually, it would be a month before he had the chance to return. Late February was still cold, but not as snowy, when he arrived in town and went into the saloon. That was when he learned two days after he left LaSalle last month, Denise had killed herself by jumping off a bridge. *Now, why would she go do a thing like that?* He was sorry she wasn't there to service him anymore. He knew he would miss that gal.

~~~

August felt the spring of 1855 was one of best times of his entire life. He had his farm, a new home, and barn. All the livestock had survived the winter and now it was time to plant.

Up before the sun and to bed long after it was gone—that was his life. He knew the hands had a hard time keeping up with him. Hard work was second nature to August, always had been. You don't accomplish anything by sitting by the fire all day.

He'd fired two hands that couldn't see why working eighteen-to-twenty-hour days were to their advantage. August hurt one of them pretty bad when he was stupid enough to badmouth him on the way off his property. *His own property!* He couldn't have that happen in front of his other hands.

Looking down, August said, "Are you dead, yet?" to the poor beaten guy on the ground and walked away. August always got the last word. That would show them punks not to get on his bad side.

The spring season was ideal and the plentiful rain brought up a perfect crop. The summer flew by quickly, as it was filled with harvest and replanting. By summer's end, August knew the Tuxhorn farm was making a name for itself. He felt he had a right to be proud.

September became the perfect Indian summer and August went into town less frequently for supplies. For the past few months, he had gone into Peru, not taking the longer route to LaSalle. There wasn't anything to entice him to the larger town anymore since poor Denise was gone, and his supply needs were getting less and less with his own crops and gardens producing.

Whenever possible, he would stop to have a drink at Horton's Pub. Sometimes he got tired of his only company being the hired help.

The waitress there was beginning to get to him. A pretty thing she was. It was the woman he had seen a year before when he rode into town about the Indian raid. She definitely caught his eye. Elizabeth Birkenbuehl was her name and she was twenty-one, only a couple of years younger than him, and also from Prussia.

They had a lot in common. She spoke his language and shared the same heritage. That was not a bad thing in itself. She had arrived in Illinois about a year ago. She said she had only been working at the pub a week when she first saw him there last year. It made him sorry he didn't come back to investigate her sooner.

There was an obvious difference between them. Elizabeth was taller than he was, by two full inches. At first it bothered him a bit, but that soon went away. With his American boots on, he was able to face her almost eye to eye. And what eyes they were. Beautiful brown eyes that seemed to have gold flecks mixed through them. They were the darnedest things August had ever seen. Those eyes against that perfect skin could make a man melt. How often he had thought of what she would look like with her hair all down.

He couldn't believe how she stayed in his thoughts. No matter what he was doing, there was that woman creeping into his mind. Elizabeth. What a pretty name.

~~~

Elizabeth's parents were Peter and Sophia Birkenbuehl, both born in Prussia during 1798. Her father was a contractor and mason. He was educated and had beautiful penmanship, making his talents in great demand in the Recorder's Office. Their entire family of thirteen children were involved in the Catholic Church back home, as was required by the government.

Elizabeth's grandfather, Matthias, was a farmer who died at the age of sixty-six in his home country. Elizabeth had been his favorite, even though he wouldn't say so directly. Her grandfather on her mother's side was Anton Heimann, a farmer and man of great influence in his community. He lived to be seventy years of age. Elizabeth knew she came from good stock.

Elizabeth was only fifteen when her mother died. It was 1848 and her mother was only fifty years old. Six years later, in 1854, Peter decided to pack up his family and head for America. She couldn't have been more excited if she tried. Her favorite brother was already there in Illinois. She poured over his letters, wanting so desperately to see him again.

The brother, Anton Birkenbuehl, was the eldest son. He had preceded the family to America in 1847, and sent letters from Illinois about the good land for farming. Anton was fourteen years older than Elizabeth and she looked up to him like she did her father.

Elizabeth was the fourth child and oldest daughter. She was needed to care for the young ones, during and after the ocean trip, since they had no mother. Unfortunately, at the age of fifty-six, her father Peter died on the trip crossing the ocean.

Now an orphan, Elizabeth only had her oldest brother, Anton, to lean on in a strange country with a strange language. He was good to her and did everything he could to make her feel welcome. In the year she had been in Illinois, she learned English along with her siblings, and slowly conformed to her new surroundings. She knew Anton was wealthy, but she insisted upon working so she could pay her own way. He agreed only if she had Sundays off to attend church with him and his family.

A stocky girl, as was desirable in her country, she had long dark hair piled up in a large, modest bun. Her pale skin offset large dark, inquisitive, eyes. She was the sort of girl to catch the eye of a fellow Prussian.

Like all of her siblings, Anton was reared by honest values and hard work. Anton Birkenbuehl helped his father in mason work when a youth, and served the required time in the Prussian Army. Wanting a better life, he immigrated to America and settled into LaSalle County, Illinois, where he wanted to spend the rest of his life.

Elizabeth still remembered the family getting the letter saying he was married on June 5, in the year of our Lord 1849. He had married Mary Katherine Hoss, daughter of Peter and

Margaret Hoss, and had four children. Two sons were lost early in their lives, leaving only one boy and one girl, for him and Mary Katherine.

But now, Anton told Elizabeth the Lord had blessed him with the responsibility of Anton's nine younger siblings. He told her they would be raised as his own children in the strict and proper way to behave in society. That was the only way it could be.

Elizabeth mothered the younger ones while the older ones went to school. Mary Katherine took over while Elizabeth worked. Their large family was doing fine.

Horton's Pub was not a saloon where men went just to get drunk. Elizabeth would never have taken a job like that. They also served suppers to the men when they were through with their work at night, if they wanted to come into town. Since alcohol was served, she made sure all patrons knew she was a waitress *only*. Anyone got out of hand with her and she would make sure they severely regretted it. The men were friendly, but no one made a fool of themselves. At least, most of them didn't.

When she was at work, she looked for August Tuxhorn to come in. Whenever he was present, she was smitten a little more each time. A small man to her, but with her being about five-feet-eight-inches tall, most men were. This one had gorgeous blue eyes, and that wavy light sandy hair was beautiful. That scar over his left eye wasn't a deterrent, quite the opposite. It seemed to make him more masculine. When he was around her, he sported a half grin that made it hard not to laugh.

He would come to see her when he could and sit until closing time. The attention was more than anything she had ever known. He would smile at her and wink when she was waiting on someone else. August was a wealthy man, having all those acres. She could sure do a lot worse. The Lord knew, he made her heart skip a beat every time she thought of him.

~~~

Fall moved into winter and August continued to see Elizabeth as often as possible, but from time to time, the weather made it more difficult. They weren't short on snow in Illinois. Some occasions made it impossible to ride into town.

He found himself missing her when that happened. He made excuses to his farmhands why he had to make trips to Peru. He was beginning to think they didn't believe him any more.

He liked Elizabeth a lot and he knew she liked him. For the first time, he thought of settling down with a woman like her. A man could sure do a lot worse. With Christmas coming up, he wanted to get her something, but not in Peru. There weren't any nice shops there. He would have to go back to LaSalle as soon as it was feasible.

Getting a weather break on Thursday, December 20, he left the farm alone and rode into LaSalle. He had no idea what he was looking for, as he had never bought a woman anything before in his life. August was the first to admit he knew nothing about women, or what they might like.

Stopping at a mercantile, he requested help from the saleslady. When August explained the present was for a female friend, there was no hesitation. She led him right to a necklace they had gotten in only the week before. It was a large cameo made of mother-of-pearl. The chain could be removed so it could be worn as a brooch.

However, the best thing about it was something he couldn't readily see. It opened into a locket. The saleslady assured him Elizabeth would love it. It was a bit pricey, but August went for it. She wrapped it for him in a pretty box with a ribbon.

On Saturday night, December 22, he went to the pub for dinner, then waited around until closing. When everyone was gone and the door locked, he walked up behind Elizabeth with the box.

"I hope you don't find me too forward, Elizabeth, but I happened to see something the other day I thought would look really nice on you." August was talking to her back.

"Whatever are you talking about?" She swung around and saw him holding the box. "August! What *have* you done?"

She quickly opened the box and stared at the necklace. When August removed it and put it around her neck, Elizabeth started to cry.

He became upset. "What's the matter, woman? Don't you like it?"

"Of course I do," she said, trying to stop the tears but not doing a very good job. "Sometimes a woman's tears are out of happiness, not sadness."

August showed her how changeable it was and then the secret of the locket. She leaned over and kissed him lightly, right on the mouth. Neither one of them could find anything to say. Realizing the sudden intimacy that had occurred, they quickly backed off from each other.

"Well, I have to be going. Merry Christmas," August said gruffly as he went out the door.

"Okay. Merry Christmas, August. I'll wear it every day!" she said to his back as he left.

~~~

True to her word, Elizabeth wore it every single day as either a necklace or a brooch, but never shared with anyone it was also a locket. She dreamed about the secrets she would put in it that no one would know about. And she dreamed of August.

Working at the pub was not easy for a single woman. Every now and then, Elizabeth would have to deal with an overly zealous drunk. This didn't worry her too much because she was not a small woman and could defend herself. From time to time, however, being the only woman who worked there could be a challenge.

One wintery night when August was not in town, a cowpoke downed too much liquor and started causing trouble. He leaned on the bar and yelled at her to "come take care of him."

Elizabeth ignored him until he pushed himself away from the bar and came up behind her. He put his arms around her waist and pulled her backward against his hardened body. He was ready to give it to her and wanted to her to know it.

It was difficult to fight off a man who was behind her, but Elizabeth kicked and yelled. A couple of other customers grabbed and pulled him off, then threw him out the door into the snow.

Elizabeth was grateful for the help of the two regulars. She thanked them for being gentlemen and bought them a drink. The night ended on an upward note.

That unfortunate event happened on a Friday night. But, before the weekend was over, that cowpoke was found dead in a creek bed outside of town with a broken neck. Everyone figured he was so drunk he fell in the creek, cracking the ice, and died. There was no reason to think anything else.

Two of August's farmhands were present and had seen the attack on Elizabeth, but were so drunk themselves, they didn't even remember telling their boss about it.

Elizabeth was just glad she wouldn't have to deal with him again.

CHAPTER NINE

Throughout the winter of 1856, she watched the door to see if her August was going to come in. He rode into town when he could, but never often enough for her. She wanted to see him all the time.

After closing, they would talk about the house he had built and the finishing touches he put on it. Then he would go into the design of the barn and how many livestock it would hold. One could assume that sort of conversation would not appeal to a woman, but it didn't matter what he talked about, Elizabeth just wanted to hear him talk. She was hopelessly in love.

In a small town like Peru, secrets were impossible to keep and rumors were the entertainment of the day. Stories were always flying about August having a tough time keeping his hired help. Working in a pub, Elizabeth was usually one of the first to hear such things. It seemed a couple of them quit because of the boss' angry tirades when something was not to his liking. One man said he was beaten up pretty bad when he accidentally left a gate open and the cows got out.

"I got 'em rounded up real quick, every one of them, but he went crazy anyway!" The poor man was hurt so badly he could hardly stand while talking.

After the pub closed that night, Elizabeth asked August about it.

"What happened with you and that hired hand? It's been all over town you beat him so bad he can hardly walk. Is that true, August?" She was holding her breath, almost afraid of the answer.

August threw his head back and laughed. "How could I have been beating this poor guy up when I was out all day gathering up the cows he was responsible for letting out? The man was a drunk and I fired him. What happened to him after that is a mystery to me."

His beautiful blue eyes twinkled as he looked at her.

Elizabeth realized she wasn't breathing and exhaled. "Well, then, let's just forget about it. I'll straighten out those gossipers if they come in here with their lies."

August gave her a tender look that melted her heart. She knew he couldn't have done it, and now she was sure. That was all she needed to hear. She told everyone that would listen, that man was a liar and August never touched him.

Elizabeth asked him one night about the scar over his left eye.

"There's nothing wrong with it, August, I was just wondering how it got there. Looks like it would have been mighty painful," she said.

August reached up and rubbed it a couple of times, then told her the story about his last fight with his old man. Elizabeth was shocked to hear about Henry's evil personality.

She was very glad to hear August had managed to get away from such torture, even if it meant he had to fight with his own father. And, to be honest, the scar made him special, different than other men.

When she heard about another employee of August's had quit for what he claimed was his boss' violent temper, she asked about it. Once again, August blamed the gossipers.

"Elizabeth, I could mention I had a sore toe at one end of town and by the time I made it to the other end, people would be saying, 'Did you hear? August lost his leg!' You know that." August and Elizabeth both laughed and the matter was over.

It was pretty obvious to Elizabeth that people were just jealous of his good looks and wealth. *Well, shame on them.*

She had, however, been present when he got into a brawl with another patron at the pub. Both men were pretty drunk, but no one stood a chance again Tuxhorn's rage. For days, talk spread about how viciously the man was beaten. Once he started, August's temper wouldn't let him stop until there wasn't much left. Elizabeth blamed it on alcohol. When two men got drunk, anything could happen. It was as simple as that.

Their affection for each other seemed to grow. It seemed they were made for each other. She could hardly believe it.

Monday was the slowest day of the week at Horton's. There was always hell raising on Saturday night and church on Sunday, which left most men tired, broke, or at home with their families on Monday night. Old man Horton didn't even come in on Mondays. He left it all in Elizabeth's capable hands.

It was on such a slow Monday, February 18, 1856. At closing time, Elizabeth locked up and started cleaning as usual, with a slightly tipsy August sitting at a table watching. She was wearing his cameo necklace. She always did.

"You're just getting prettier and prettier, Elizabeth." August slurred his words a little, but he had a charming smile. He was leaning his chair backward toward the wall behind him, with one foot balanced upon another chair, gently rocking himself.

"I hear that all day long, August. Tell me something I don't know." She sounded gruff, but they both knew she didn't mean it. Actually, she was flattered, as usual, by August's attention.

"Okay." August thought a few seconds. "How 'bout 'I think of you all the time?' Does that work?"

They both laughed out loud at his slightly silly response and then there was a silence between them for a long moment as they just looked at each other.

August stood up from the table and walked over to her. Then he was standing close. Very close. Elizabeth felt his arm slide around her waist and gently pull her even closer. Elizabeth wasn't about to fight this man off.

He kissed her softly and looked into her eyes. When she looked back into his, it was easy to forget the painful loss of her parents, the never-ending years of being mother to her young siblings, and the long hours she worked every day at the pub.

Right now—this very moment—she was a woman, a desirable woman. Walking with him into the back room, Elizabeth Birkenbuehl shut the door behind them. It was there she submitted to August Tuxhorn.

In the coming days, Elizabeth knew she was in love. She was totally, completely, happily in love. August was her knight in shining armor, the one who would sweep her away from the boring life she had now. Of course August loved her. Why else would he have spent so much time with her or bought her the necklace? And that night. That night when he made her realize the love she had for him.

For the first two weeks after their back room encounter, Elizabeth was floating on cloud nine. Yes, she was in love. How tender and sweet August had been when he touched her. How loving and gentle. After all these years, she would finally have the love she so desperately needed.

Everyone who came into the pub saw the difference in her. When they asked her what was up, she would always smile and say, "Spring is in the air." In early March, that was not exactly the case, but no one was going to argue with her over it.

It was toward the end of March, about the end of a four-week span, when she noticed August hadn't come back to see her at all. During the first couple of weeks, this was not a concern, for she knew he would be fighting the weather and planning to get the spring planting done on time. Even though he had hired several more farmhands to keep up, it was a busy time of the year for any farmer, let alone one with a lot of acreage.

"Whatever could be keeping him?" she wondered out loud while cleaning up each night. "I know he loves me. He is probably just as shook up about our love as I am.

"He is going to walk in here soon and just march right up to me and ask me to be his bride!" Elizabeth kept that thought in her mind every day.

She was going to be the wife of a wealthy farmer. Her momma and daddy would have been so proud! How she wished they could have been here for her wedding.

It was about mid-April when her thoughts of love and marriage were slowly fading into panic. Where was he? Why hadn't he come back to see her? After two months, Elizabeth knew he would have had the time to come and see her—if he wanted to. But why wouldn't he want to? What could be going on?

More days passed, with no sign of August. Then it became painfully clear he was avoiding her. Her heart broke. She was very angry at herself for her schoolgirl stupidity and angry at him for his cruel betrayal. That night in February wasn't right—she knew that—but it wasn't wrong either. They had both wanted each other.

After three months went by with no sight of August, Elizabeth knew she had been used and thrown away. He got what he wanted from her and now she wasn't good enough for him. Her emotions settled into bitterness and all that incredible love turned into a bounty of hate.

~~~

It was June before August dared to stop into the pub again, but he was no longer interested in Elizabeth. She had proven herself to be a whore and he didn't need that kind of woman. Oh, he had taken her virginity, he knew that. But to let a man touch her before marriage—what kind of woman would do that?

"I mean, if she would do that with me, how many others will have their way with her?" August ran that scenario over and over in his mind until his feelings for her were nothing more than contempt. He had been so wrong about her.

Pretty, yes, but those gold-flecked brown eyes weren't enough to forget what she had done. Oh, he had great memories of that night, but they were soured by the fact that she would let a man take her without marriage. It wasn't right and he knew it.

The few times he went to the pub again, he never looked at nor spoke to her, and always left well before closing. Nor did she talk to him when he was there.

"She's probably already humping some other guy by now." August was glad to get away from her. Elizabeth was no good and he felt lucky to have found out before he did something stupid like marrying her!

August knew her brother, Anton Birkenbuehl, very well. Who didn't? He was well established in the county, with easy friendships with judges and councilmen. He was a wealthy man to be reckoned with, a hard worker with a good farm and the respect of one and all.

One never knew; maybe August would need a contact like that one of these days. He sure didn't want to cross the man. He was glad no one, especially Anton, knew what had happened between Elizabeth and him. He would just as soon forget about it himself. It just never happened. From now on, he would stick to professionals.

CHAPTER TEN

Since having arrived in Illinois over two years ago, August had built a good solid farmstead, including a nice house completely furnished and a large barn with pens for the horses and cows. The chicken house was supplying all the eggs he and his hands could eat. A large garden behind the house was yielding the needed vegetables. Fruit trees were still growing but would produce in a few more years.

He currently had nine farmhands working for him, staying in the adjoining bunkhouse built off the side of the barn. Only three beds were in there the first summer, but this spring, seven more arrived and he had more than enough to keep all them off the floor. That surely made things better. He would keep ordering those beds until he had fifteen in there, like he said he would.

A lot of his place was in crop and the rest in grazing. August had made some acquaintances with his closest neighbors, but mostly stayed to himself. He was feeling pretty good about it all. It felt right to be left alone and have everything a man could want.

It amused him to think about the family he left in Prussia. *What losers.* He had more than they could ever imagine having. He thought back to his father's one cow and horse. He should have one of them "pictures" taken of his place and send it to them, but he feared they would show up on his doorstep expecting to move in. He would never allow that to happen.

It was too bad about Elizabeth. He had really cared for her and thought she was proper. Obviously, that was not the case. It was her fault, not his. He knew that. He was just being a man, but she was a loose woman. Not the kind of woman that a man would want to marry.

August mostly avoided going to the pub. He went once in a while, but he finally figured out he wasn't going to find a nice respectable girl in a pub. He also made sure he got home early. The farm was all that mattered now.

It was Friday, July 25, in 1856. Everyone was up before dawn. One of the hands cooked everyone a big breakfast and now it was time for the chores. August was thinking about riding over to the west twenty to check on the amount of water that was still in his lake. In this heat, he had to make sure there was enough water for the animals.

He stepped out onto the covered front porch of his house, taking in the fresh morning air as he watched the sun start to rise. It was beautiful. He had a good life and he was proud of all he had accomplished in such a short time.

He couldn't be more content.

Hearing horse hooves, August spotted Anton Birkenbuehl as he rode up to his farmhouse. *Whatever is he doing here?* He did not look happy. The intense anger in his face took August aback. *What could possibly be wrong, and why is he here?*

Dismounting his horse almost before it came to a stop, Anton swung his fist and made contact on August's left eye. Down he went. Anton grabbed him off the ground by his neck, slamming his back into a post on his new porch. Being six feet tall made it easy for Anton, especially since his actions had taken August by surprise. When he spoke, August saw spit flying from his mouth.

"Why did you ruin my sister? How could you do that to *me?* I have been nothing but nice to you since you arrived. My own countryman would take a woman *before her vows?*"

It was obvious Anton was beside himself with anger. August went white in the face. How could Anton possibly know? Who would have told him? Why would Eliza—?

The thought hit him so hard, it was like a horse fell on his chest. The pain in his mind was worse than his newly developing black eye. Elizabeth must be...pregnant. *Sie können nicht ernst sein!*

Anton got right to the point. "Your bastard child isn't going to ruin my family. Do you hear me? I have worked too hard, to let the likes of you tarnish my family's reputation."

August doubted Anton had ever been this angry in his life. His sister was with child and not married. It was obvious to August that he hated them both.

"You caused this problem, Tuxhorn, and you are going to fix it. And you will fix it *now!* The Birkenbuehl name is not going to be ruined by a slimy dog like you. Tomorrow you will go into town with Elizabeth and get a marriage license. You both will then say your vows before a judge. You will make her a respectable woman and no one can know of her condition! *Is that clear?*"

There wasn't much talking August could do. Amazingly, he realized not a word Anton said was in a raised voice. It just sounded like he had shouted from the hilltop.

Hardly able to breathe with Anton still holding him by the throat, August managed to choke out, "Tomorrow is Satur—"

Anton didn't wait for him to finish. "The Clerk's Office will be open *just for you,* Tuxhorn. Just for you and Elizabeth. I will see to it."

August knew there was no getting out of this and nodded. He had not even had time to get the news of Elizabeth's pregnancy around his brain, and now he would be forced to marry her?

Anton threw him down on the ground and got back on his horse before he said, "I will be by with a buggy at daylight to pick you up to go into town. And you had better be ready, in your very best suit of clothes, Tuxhorn. You had *better* be ready." Anton rode away just as fast as he came.

August wasn't afraid of any man, but he had been completely blindsided by the unexpected. He knew Anton wanted to kill him. There was no denying it was in his eyes. Like it or not, he was going to have to make it right.

He walked back into his house and slammed the door behind him. The hired hands would be working without him today.

The following morning, a stern-faced Anton pulled up in a buggy. In the backseat was Elizabeth with red swollen eyes. It looked as if she had been crying for days. Her misery was belied by the pretty dress and matching bonnet she was wearing.

With the painful black eye Anton had given him, August came out of his house in the one suit he owned. Though Elizabeth did not even look his way, he glared at her with hatred and got into the buggy. Not a sound was made by any of them all the way to town.

As predicted, the Clerk's Office was open for Anton and the paperwork filled out for the marriage license. Standing behind a counter, the clerk prepared the papers and slid them toward him. August struggled when told to sign the forms. He noticed Elizabeth didn't fare much better.

August could see on the face of the clerk that he was taking in the tension of the people in front of him. He wondered what the clerk was thinking. But then again, he didn't even know what he was thinking, himself.

The clerk quietly and quickly got the paperwork together, and handed Anton the marriage license. He handed it to Anton, not to the people getting married. As they left the office, August heard the door close and lock behind them.

The next stop was back out to Anton's place where his friend, a traveling judge, gave the nuptials. Anton was best man and his wife, Mary Katherine, stood as matron of honor. As soon as "I now pronounce you man and wife" was spoken, Elizabeth's bags were put in the back of the buggy.

She was crying again as she said her goodbyes to her young siblings, who looked up to her as a mother. Now Mary Katherine would be their mother.

Anton drove the newlyweds back to August's farm, dropped them off, and left. During this entire time, August realized Anton had not spoken to either one, nor had they spoken with him or each other.

~~~

Finally alone, the shock of the last twenty-four hours was beginning to settle on her. Elizabeth had lost the love of her dear brother and her reputation due to her actions. Now she was married to a man she hated and was carrying a child she didn't want. From what she could see, August felt the same about her. To think she had actually loved him once. How could that have happened?

Without a word, August set her bags inside the house and turned to leave. He went to the barn for his horse and rode away. Elizabeth was relieved to see him leave. She could at least be able to unpack in peace.

She had dreamed of marrying August and settling into this new farmhouse to have a family. Now that it was real, she found it was not the pleasure she had thought it would be. All she felt was hate.

~~~

August knew he had to leave the house. Truth be known, if he had stayed that first night, he probably would have killed her for destroying his perfect life. Of course, if he had killed her, then Anton would surely have hunted him down and done the same.

"August, ol' boy, you can't win, can you? No matter what you do, you can't win." He was talking to the crickets. Sitting up against a tree, he took a deep swig of the bottle he had started. The more he drank, the less he could stand the thought of his new wife.

That trollop had ruined everything. Now he was stuck with her and her brat. He didn't even know if that kid was his. It could belong to any of the guys that hung out in the pub. Why did he have to suffer for *her* mistakes?

His campfire was flickering out as he looked over the lake next to the rolling hills of his land. The sky was dark blue and peaceful as it began twinkling with starlight. Hills were bathed in gold and scarlet, displaying the stunning last breath of an Illinois summer sun.

But August didn't care. Why should he? His life was ruined. He finished the bottle and lay down. It was time to get some sleep.

The following morning, he felt awful, but couldn't tell if it was because he was hungover or because he had married a harlot. Either way, it was not going to be a good day. One thing was sure. He wasn't going to take any crap from her.

Riding back to his farmhouse, the new groom had no emotion on his face. He found Elizabeth in the kitchen. She swung to face him as he walked into the house.

August spoke in a low voice seething with anger. "You will cook and clean every day. You will make sure everything is spotless. You will never question my authority. You will submit to me whenever I want. Is all of this perfectly clear?"

Stunned, Elizabeth stared at him a moment and then, without a word, turned and walked away.

~~~

August had been gone all night and Elizabeth didn't care. She needed the time to get a grip on the turn her life had taken. She decided to rearrange things in the kitchen to better fit her height. That was when she heard him. He slammed the door as he entered the house and she swung to face him.

He gave his little spiel about what she would or wouldn't do while she just stood staring at him. Elizabeth couldn't believe he was angry at *her*.

I am the one who should be angry! I am the innocent woman he had taken advantage of. I am the one who had been thrown away like I was trash. He is the one who put this child inside of me. This is his fault. She stared wide-eyed at this hideous stranger standing in front of her.

It was all she could do to keep from getting into a physical altercation with him. Elizabeth clenched her teeth and fists. She was sure she was going to kill him with her bare hands. At this point, however, there weren't a lot of options. She couldn't go back to her brother's house, nor could she continue working while in a family way. They glared into each other's eyes; then, without answering, Elizabeth turned and walked away.

The days stretched into weeks and they barely spoke. Elizabeth would have meals on the table and leave, so he ate alone. She would eat when he wasn't in the house. They ignored each other as much as possible.

In the fall, as her time was approaching, Anton's wife, Mary Katherine, would ride over once a week to help out, and keep her company. Elizabeth knew Anton didn't mind if his wife wanted to come visit, but she also knew he couldn't forgive her. He, no doubt, compared her to his sweet and caring wife who always did the right thing. A comparison she would always fail miserably.

"You will feel so different after the baby is born, Elizabeth. You will love that darling little thing." Mary Katherine hated to see anyone down. She brought baby blankets, a cradle, and other infant items they no longer needed for their children.

"Don't worry about Anton, dear," she said. "He will get over all this with time. He was taken by surprise, is all."

Taken by surprise? Mary, dear, don't you think I was, too? Elizabeth wanted to say something, but thought it best not to at this point. Her sister-in-law was her only visitor and friend. She didn't want to run her off; besides, she was stuck in this cruel life and there was nothing anyone could do about it.

"I hope you are right, Mary," Elizabeth finally said with deep sadness. "I just can't imagine my life without my brother."

"Of course I'm right. Anton loves you. You'll see." Mary Katherine was an optimist.

Whenever August came home and Mary Katherine was present, Elizabeth knew he would be very nice. He didn't want any bad news going back to Anton. Just another sign he was a manipulator.

She didn't want this baby—or its father. The initial hate finally settled into a cold resolve. As Mrs. August Tuxhorn, her fate was set, but her heart was closed off. She would never be hurt again. When a person showed they care, they got slapped in the face. *Well, no more.* She would never give her heart to any one or any thing again.

~~~

August never touched her while she was carrying this child, but he made sure she was very aware with every passing day that he found her fat and disgusting. His drinking was also increasing. He needed it so he didn't have to think about her and how she had ruined his life.

On Wednesday, November 19, 1856, August came home from the fields and found Mary Katherine there. It was unusual for mid-week, but he soon discovered Elizabeth was in labor, about to give birth. *Great, guess that means she won't have my supper ready.*

August stayed on the front porch. He didn't want to be a part of what was going on inside. He heard the screams—how could he not? *It hurts? It serves you right.* Shortly after dark, Mary Katherine came out and told him he had a son. Charles Henry Tuxhorn had been born. He didn't care. He didn't want either one of them.

CHAPTER ELEVEN

August was hard on Charles, but he noticed Elizabeth was, too. That woman was cold as ice. How could he have ever cared so much for her? It was obvious she didn't have maternal feelings for the boy. Well, he wasn't about to coddle the kid, either. *He needs to learn to look out for himself, like I did.*

With the years, additional babies were born. Fights among him and Elizabeth were common and physical. The misery in the house was palatable.

He took his rage mostly out on the children. He knew they were afraid of him and that was the way he liked it. He couldn't stand the sight of them, and would kick them out of his way, when he walked by.

August bragged about how he got the scar over his left eye and how he had taken on Henry and won. He wanted those brats to know he could, and would, take on anyone.

Elizabeth was a problem, though. She physically fought back. He hadn't seen that one coming. When he hit her, he had to expect she was going to punch him back. He had to admit there were times when pure chaos reigned in the household.

Four years after Charles was born, the American Civil War started. At first, August was livid. He thought he had left war behind.

But as the politics in Illinois came into play, he was forced to pay attention to what was going on around him. The North was fighting the South because the North didn't want Negroes enslaved any longer. The South was fighting the North because the South wanted to enslave Negroes. None of this mattered to him one whit, but the nature of the politics was hard, if not impossible, to ignore.

~~~

The war only lasted five years, but they were hazardous years, even as far north as Illinois. As a northern state and the one the president came from, Abraham Lincoln was strongly supported by Governor Richard Yates, but the strongly Democratic legislature sympathized with the South. It was a treacherous time and people were afraid to declare where their sympathies lay because they feared they would be talking to a murderer of the opposite persuasion. People did get killed for their opinion. August knew it was a good thing he didn't have one.

From time to time, people went missing and most knew it was because of their personal beliefs. August just wanted to make sure this Civil War foolishness didn't bother him or his farm. He never declared support for either side. It wasn't a ploy; he really didn't care one way or the other.

By early 1863, there was a complete breakdown of relations between the Republican governor and the Democratic majority in the legislature. The 1863 session of the Illinois General Assembly was filled with fireworks and ended with an action never seen before—or since.

In February, Republican Senator Funk gave a scathing speech that brought the session to an end. As the legislature prepared to recess, the actions by the anti-war majority brought the senator to white heat. The McLean County legislator announced that he would happily serve as judge, jury, and executioner against those fellow legislators that he saw as enemies of the United States:

Mr. Speaker, you must excuse me; I could sit no longer in my seat and listen to these traitors. My heart... would not let me. My heart, that cries out for the lives of our brave volunteers in the field, that these traitors at home are destroying by thousands, would not let me. My heart, that bleeds for the widows and the orphans at home, would not let me. Yes, these traitors and villains in the Senate are killing my neighbors' boys, now fighting in the field.

Mr. Speaker, these traitors on this floor should be provided with hempen collars. They deserve them. They deserve hanging, I say.... I go for hanging them, and I dare to tell them so, right here, to their traitorous faces. Traitors should be hung. It would be the salvation of the country to hang them.

Funk's speech caused a sensation, astonishing some and bringing cheers from others in the galleries. It was reported or quoted at length in newspapers throughout the northern states and was even issued in pamphlet form in both English and German.

The legislature became so inflamed over the emancipation issue that they had to recess until June to let tempers cool. When they finally reconvened, the governor declared the session closed just after it started and all Republicans got up and left. This action ended the possibility of the Democrats getting any legislation through to keep slavery alive in Illinois.

The Democrats sued the governor, but his ability to end a session of his own accord was upheld. As governor, Yates had the power to back Lincoln and prevent "traitors" from determining policy in Illinois.

By the time the war was over, Illinois was firmly ensconced behind the Emancipation Proclamation. August was glad they finally came to a decision, whatever it was.

~~~

Charles wasn't aware of the trouble in the land. As a small boy, he was fighting a war in his own home. He did remember the war ended when he was nine. He spent his young years in Illinois, avoiding his mother and father as much as possible. He really didn't understand why they hated him so much until he was about eight years old.

A boy at school had called his mother names. Charles was not stupid. He now knew what had happened. His mother was a loose woman and he was the result. Like his father, he could hardly stand the thought of the woman who was his mother. But he couldn't see the bad blood between father and son ever ceasing, either.

Charles knew no one, including his father, doubted his parentage. He had his mother's dark hair, but he was the spitting image of August, staring back at him with the same large blue eyes.

As he grew older, he knew there was anger in him that defied explanation. He didn't see it in others, not for more than a moment or two, anyway. He couldn't understand why he had this need to strike out; a need to hurt, just to make it through the day.

Some said he possessed a worse temper than his father, if that was possible. Charles knew what was said about him, but, again, he didn't care. He lacked respect for anything or anyone unless it ultimately benefitted him. Why should he?

He certainly learned when to smile and be charming. Charles knew how to manipulate people; to do what was necessary to obtain what he wanted. He learned early in life if he didn't like something or someone, just threaten it, beat it into submission, or kill it. They worked well for him.

His father only spoke to his children in anger, apparently unable to stand the sight of any of them. He was abusive mentally, as well as physically. A wrong look could get a child hit across the face, so they looked down when he was around.

Charles figured if the buzzard stopped drinking, he might have some control over his life.

The boys learned to farm very early in life, while the girls learned to clean and cook from Elizabeth. Charles noticed his mother wasn't quite as hard on his other siblings as she was on him, but he didn't care. Why would he care about what a whore thought?

Charles knew he was good-looking and would most likely grow into a very handsome man. In fact, when it came to height and looks, the son could put his father to shame. Taking after his mother's family, he was already taller than his father hitting five feet seven, at fourteen-years-old. His dark hair and blueberry eyes stood out like jewels on a crown. When he smiled, it could light up a room. That is, when he wanted it to. All these assets he put to good use.

Charles had to grin, thinking about his looks. They sure didn't help him a few days ago when he was caught by his father in the act of killing one of their hunting dogs. None of the dogs liked him. They always growled and tried to bite him. This particular dog was the worst. He had enticed it over with a raw piece of rabbit .

Once it came close enough, Charles grabbed it around its neck and ran a knife across its throat. He figured that should teach it a lesson. He's fourteen now and was tired of being the butt end for everyone else. Wouldn't you know it? Just as he was dropping the dead creature, his father walked into the barn.

"What have you done, you slimeball!" August was beside himself. "You killed MY dog! You filthy—"

The old man lunged for him. Charles knew his father wanted to kill him. He grabbed the closest thing to him and watched as August came at him. Charles swung and hit him over the head with the back of a pitchfork.

Leaning over his nearly unconscious father, Charles' own hate came pouring out. "If you ever touch me again, I will kill you. Got that? Don't ever come near me again."

His father seemed to believe him, because he hadn't spoken to him since. Charles was actually proud of taking a stand against his father. He could kick himself for not doing it years earlier. *Wasn't he the one that was always bragging about taking on his own father? Well, now it's my turn.* One thing was for sure, no one was ever going to get the best of him again.

For the next two weeks, the hatred between father and son was palatable. The others dared not look at either one of them for fear of getting hit.

~~~

August could not believe what Charles had done. How dare he kill a hunting dog? *That hunting dog that belonged to me!* As he struggled to get up off of the barn floor, he rolled over to get his bearings. He was bleeding and his head was killing him.

He was alone in the barn. No, there was the dog—lifeless. Blood was everywhere. He tried to sit up, when he remembered what happened. Charles had hit him and knocked him out. How much of this blood was his? He was out of control, that boy. August was not going to be pushed around by a punk, no matter how big he got.

The memory of taking on his father came rushing back. The shock of it was almost more than he could bear, and his mind refused to compare the two incidences.

Holding the back of his head, he noticed the pitchfork. The pitchfork. More memories came flooding back of the last moments with his mother. He had thrown a pitchfork at her, but missed. He couldn't remember now if he had actually meant to hit her, or not. That was such a long time ago. None of that mattered anyway. He had bigger problems.

Now *he* had a son who thought he was better than his father. Completely out of control, he was. August knew he couldn't live like his father—with a son he had no control over. He was better than Henry and wasn't going to stand for it.

He thought about all of the other children. It seemed like they never stopped showing up. How many did he have now? Not sure how many and really didn't care. One was too many for him.

August knew how much Elizabeth hated him touching her, so it gave him pleasure to demand it. But, being of good German stock, she kept getting pregnant. She would keep bearing children because he had the last word. He always got the last word. Something his oldest son seemed to have forgotten.

About two weeks after his conflict with Charles, August was in town when a calvary unit rode into Peru. It was the spring of 1870, and they were on their way to Fort Scott, Kansas.

August was buying the captain a drink in the pub, learning all about their intended destination. Old man Horton had passed on years back, and it was now just called The Pub, by its new owners.

The captain told him the Army was returning because of the formation of a post in southeast Kansas. The post was based at Fort Scott, Kansas, but the soldiers camped along the rail tracks, and seldom used the original fort.

They returned to protect the railroads, and workers from settlers who feared the railroad, which had been awarded land by the United States government in right-of-ways, would evict them from their squatter homes. The settlers considered the troops lackeys to the railroads and lumped both as enemies. By 1870, more troops were needed to control both sides.

After about an hour of chatting, August brought up an idea he was working on.

"Say, Captain," August said as he refilled the captain's shot glass. "How about you take my boy with you to Kansas? I would pay you for your time and trouble and he would sure be a help to you folks. He's real good at taking care of horses."

"Why would he want to go to Kansas, Tuxhorn?"

August noticed the captain didn't seem to be against the idea, but he was surprised at the comment.

"He's always had a wandering heart. You know what I mean. Seems some boys are like that. Guess I was that way myself, since I came over the ocean and all." August was wearing his

MURDER IS A FAMILY AFFAIR

'father-wants-what's-best-for-son' face and it was obvious to him that the captain was falling for it.

"Yeah, I do understand. Kinda that way myself, I guess. Fine with me, Tuxhorn, but we leave in exactly eight days and I can't wait a moment longer."

"You won't have to, I promise." August drew out a quick map to his farm.

"We'll be there about noon. He'll have to have his own mount. Have his stuff ready to go by then." The captain thought it might be fun to have a young eager fellow riding with them.

"You won't be sorry. He is a good worker." August was so pleased with himself he could hardly stand it.

For the next eight days, August was almost happy. He and Charles continued to ignore each other, but the father was about to prove he was still the one in charge.

On the morning it was all to come down, Charles had saddled his horse and left early. To go where, he didn't say. He never did anymore. After he rode off, August told Elizabeth to pack up all of Charles' things immediately and have them ready before noon. He noticed even Elizabeth was too confused to talk back and did what she was told.

The military unit rode in about 11:30 a.m. August burst out the door and welcomed them with open arms. Charles rode back to the house at that very moment and was about to get off his horse, but hesitated. August ignored Charles, and spoke of him as if he wasn't even present.

"You will like my boy's help, Captain. He can work hard." August reached up to shake the Captains hand then handed him a pouch of gold coins with the agreed upon sum.

Charles looked stunned when his mother came out with a bag of his belongings. It had not quite dawned on him what was taking place. Probably the only time in his life he couldn't think straight.

"What's going on? What 'boy' will....That's my—"

August thought he would laugh out loud at his surprised son's blubbering.

~~~

This can't be happening, Charles thought. *I will kill that rotten slimeball. I won't do it...*

However, leaving actually sounded good to Charles. Maybe this was how to get away from these miserable people. He had just returned from spending the morning riding around the farm, wondering what he wanted to do with his life and how to do it. Maybe this was his answer. He could leave.

The war was over, so maybe the military... He had never known any place but Peru, Illinois. What else was out there? Thoughts tumbled quickly over and over as he still sat in the saddle, totally dumbstruck.

His things were thrown into the supply wagon and, at the age of fourteen, Charles turned his horse around and rode away with the military unit.

He knew he would never have to see, or speak, to his father again, and that was a very pleasing thought as he rode away. He never looked back.

~~~

The family watched as Charles rode away with the soldiers. August was in a very good mood. He knew he was back in charge and no kid of his was going to get the better of him again. He would have to make sure they all got the message.

Charles was almost out of sight when August turned to go to the barn. His son, Leo, was in his way. At four-years-old, he was already becoming a nuisance. August swung his hand and slapped him up the side of the head as he walked by. He heard the brat scream. It felt good.

August Tuxhorn always had the last word.

PART TWO
CHARLES HENRY TUXHORN

CHAPTER TWELVE

*T*his could actually work out, Charles thought. *Finally getting to leave everyone behind is just fine with me.*

No matter that his father had sold him down the river—leaving actually sounded good to Charles. He was fourteen now, after all. He was no longer a kid who had to take someone else's orders. He hated taking orders. Really.

He had wondered what to do with his life for the past year or so, and had thought about leaving. Nonetheless, it was a shock to see his mother put all of his earthly belongings into some military wagon. They didn't have to force him to leave, though. He hated them all and wanted nothing more than to get out.

Within a few days of riding with the military, Charles was enchanted by all the new things he saw. He couldn't believe his eyes. The farther south they went, the warmer the temperatures were. Spring was in full bloom. Trees greened, flowers bloomed, and creeks were rushing with water from the melted snow. He figured this would be worth exploring.

To get the information he needed, Charles was very polite to the military men. He asked about Fort Scott, the people, and the opportunities in Kansas. What about Missouri? What could he do to support himself?

Hours of talking around campfires paid off. They informed him Missouri was prettier and had a better climate than Kansas. The farther west one went, the hotter it got, they told him.

Missouri had lots of water for good crops and cattle. He was told a boy like himself could earn a living by working on a farm. He would get room and board and some wages, too. Being a hired farm worker in Missouri didn't sound too bad to Charles. Until he could get his own place, and be the boss, that is.

They had travelled about 500 miles to the southwest when they pulled into Nevada, Missouri. It was a sight to see. This was what Charles was looking for. As he expressed his desire to stay to his new military buddies, he was told it hadn't always been this nice.

The captain said it was just five years ago, at the end of the Civil War, that Vernon County had pretty much been burned to the ground. Actually, the year 1863 was "the most woeful" in its history.

"Back and forth into Missouri rode the Kansas Jayhawkers, back and forth into Kansas rode the Missouri guerrillas, back and forth into loyal Cedar rode the Vernon Bushwhackers, back and forth into rebel Vernon rode the Cedar militia," the captain said.

Charles listened as several of the troops related the story; each seemed to take up where the others left off. He learned that Montevallo was burned by Iowa troops on April 14, 1862.

"Farms were burned and pillaged. Men and boys were slain. Normal life, schooling, churches, and law courts had become a dim memory. The few families who hadn't fled south, struggling to carry on in a normal way, had a hard time of it. They were preyed upon by both sides," said a standing soldier named Fred.

They told him the climax came on May 26, 1863. One hundred Federal militiamen from Cedar and St. Clair Counties under Captain Anderson Morton burned Nevada in revenge for a Bushwhacker ambush on a militia party on the Nevada square, resulting in the deaths of two militiamen.

"The militiamen were erroneously convinced the Nevadans gave the Bushwhackers support and information. They called the town 'the Bushwhacker capitol.' Some seventy-five homes and all public buildings, save the schoolhouse and jail, were burned. Only half a dozen small houses were spared," the captain said.

The soldier sitting next to the captain continued, "When the war ended in the spring of 1865, all Vernon County lay devastated. Hardly a hundred families remained, and all the towns, with the partial exception of Balltown, had been destroyed. Few farms were left untouched. Kansas Jayhawkers had stolen even the fence rails. Public businesses, untended for four years, were in hopeless disorder."

It certainly wasn't what Charles was seeing now.

Another soldier jumped in with, "After the war, many of the landowners and soldiers from both sides who were still alive came home to start rebuilding. In a short five years, Nevada had a new county courthouse and a population of about twelve hundred citizens. Vernon County had new homes, farms repopulated, crops planted, and livestock replaced. Businesses were thriving and there was a lot of land to be had if a person had the money."

The captain finished their story by saying, "This place is ripe for a young boy dreaming of getting rich."

Charles had no problem deciding to stay in Missouri.

The next day, he said goodbye to the unit heading on to Fort Scott. He walked the town, wondering what to do, when he spotted the Sheriff's Office. Walking through the door, he was stopped by a deputy who wanted to know the nature of his business. The sheriff, T.B. Brown, looked up and listened.

"I am looking for work. About anything will do, but I know how to work on a farm."

Sheriff Brown spoke up and said, "Dave, I'll take care of this." He questioned Charles as to why he was alone and where he came from.

Charles looked him right in the eye and said, "I am an orphan. My parents died on their way here in a covered wagon. I came in with some soldiers who happened by. I can take care of myself, sir. Don't you worry about that."

The sheriff said to come back in the morning and he would see what he could do. Then he reached into his pocket, gave the boy a dime, and told him to go get something to eat. Charles was grateful. Not grateful enough to trust him, however. He would never trust anyone again. Ever.

Charles curled up in the livery for the night. The following morning, he was at the Sheriff's Office early. The sheriff seemed impressed by that.

"Son, I have some good friends, Mr. and Mrs. Amos Walters, and they tell me they need another farmhand on their sixty acres. You think you would be able to handle it?"

"Yes, sir. I can do it. They won't be sorry." Charles was excited for the chance.

The sheriff rode him out to the Walters' place and introduced them. Amos Walters hired him on the spot and had Charles make himself a bed in their barn. He was finally on his own. Regular meals and some wages made life sound pretty good.

CHAPTER THIRTEEN

Charles learned a lot spending his teen years in Vernon County, Missouri. He continued learning how to farm, what to look for in a good horse or heifer, and what to avoid when purchasing a bull. Amos Walters taught him what to do in a civil manner and treated him with respect. It was a way of life he had never known before. It was so different, Charles didn't trust it. *Never let your guard down or they will get the best of you. Don't trust anyone.*

The last time he let his guard down, his old man had sold him down the river. No, that was not about to happen again. If there was only one lesson a man had to learn in his life, that would be it. Trust no one.

Now that he was grown, it was amusing to look back on his life here in Missouri. He wasn't very good at holding his temper, but that had always worked to his advantage. There was just something inside him that wanted to strike out, the harder the better. Sometimes, it even surprised him.

He saved most of his earnings as a farmhand, meager as they were. He didn't want for anything—food or shelter—so why throw the money away? He was amazed at how many of the hired help in the county would end up drunk on Saturday night and broke on Sunday. They were weak and worthless. Drunken bums like his old man. Charles stayed in control of his mind. He was always in charge.

That didn't mean he didn't get in trouble. Charles figured it must follow him around. He would fight a person who even looked at him crooked. He wouldn't stand for anything that even hinted of disrespect.

He knew his excellent work for Amos was what kept him out of jail on many occasions. The old guy would stand up for him with the sheriff. With his temper seemingly increasing, the other hands gave him a wide berth, which was exactly the way he wanted it.

Fear got him all the respect he felt he deserved. He didn't need any more than that. At the age of nineteen, Charles was in town on an errand for his boss. He was near the stables, about to round a corner. He stopped dead in his tracks when he heard his name spoken. He backed up a couple of feet so he could hear, but not be seen.

"You gotta stay away from that Tuxhorn kid," the blacksmith was telling some local rancher. "He's a mean one, he is. Best to avoid him altogether."

Charles almost chuckled at the comment. He wanted folks to be afraid of him. That was the only way he would get the respect that was rightfully his. What really set him off came next.

"That punk don't scare me, none. He's all bluster, he is. Thinks he has something to prove. Well, if he wants to try me, I'll let my dogs have him. Then I'll bury what's left in my cornfield!"

Charles never made his presence known to the pair in the stables, but the rancher found all of his dogs dead the next morning. He would bet that big-mouth wouldn't accuse him of being all bluster, again. It truly was a fond memory.

~~~

Throughout his time spent in Vernon County, there wasn't a sheriff that didn't know the name of Charles Tuxhorn. His reputation was one of charm and violence. He used charm to get what he wanted, and violence if that didn't work. A new sheriff would be warned about Charles before he even pinned on the badge.

Sheriff Wallar was no exception. He knew the man's actions were mean, despicable, and generally illegal. But no matter how he tried to arrest Tuxhorn, paid off or frightened "witnesses" always gave him an alibi.

He was a young weasel who thought the world owed him something. Well, not so young any more. He figured Charles was about twenty-three now, only six years younger than himself. Hopefully, one day, a Vernon County sheriff would stop him. At least, that was the plan, and Wallar was hoping he would be that sheriff.

It was frustrating. As mean as Charles was, his good looks still got him the attention of all the ladies, even some married ones. And getting them to meet him in places where clothes could be removed without being seen, didn't seem to be a problem either. The sheriff knew Charles was asking for trouble. Begging for it, really.

If some husband blew him away, would I even arrest him? The killer would be doing the town a public service, wouldn't he? That's the way the sheriff saw it. At least the thought made him smile.

Charles' reputation as a ladies man lasted longer than most of his relationships, due to his temper. It seemed the frightened ladies would decide another man, maybe not so attractive, would be much better suited for them. The sheriff wished more women saw it that way.

A lady no longer being available didn't seem to matter much to Charles. There was always more ladies willing to fall prey to his looks and charm. *What is it that guy has that no woman can seem to help but fall all over him?*

Sheriff Wallar was sick of Tuxhorn, but he wasn't going to let it ruin his breakfast. His Molly said she would have it ready soon, so he was going to walk back to their house, only a block away from his office.

Leaving his deputy in charge, he left the Sheriff's Office and started down the street. *Molly is a wonderful cook and I can't get enough of her biscuits. I can't get enough of her, either. I have been so lucky to be the one to get her heart. She is one fine woman and...*

Someone was screaming! Sheriff Wallar swung around and started running back toward his office. He saw a man swing off his horse and stood waiting for him, with tears running down his face. A grown man was crying. What could have happened?

Getting a hold of the man and shaking him a bit, he learned a girl had been badly beaten out at Tent and he needed to hurry out there with the doc.

His deputy had come out the office door. As Wallar mounted his horse, he turned to him and yelled, "You get the doc and get out to Tent fast! I'm on my way."

Tent was what the locals called Tent Town. It was an area where poor folks set up tents or other unstable living quarters and worked as work was available. Whole families lived outside of Nevada in their own community.

A couple of times per year, the townsfolk of Nevada would gather for a bake sale or horse race to help raise money for the poor in Tent. Oh, they didn't give money to the poor slob that didn't want to work, or preferred to stay drunk. The money was given to store owners, doctors and dentists in town. They would take whatever amount they had been given and remove that amount from ongoing accounts owed him by the poor folks. Their generosity helped pay on doctor bills and grocery debts for those living in Tent Town. Sometimes, whole debts were paid off.

If it weren't for the people of Nevada's kindness toward them, many more would have died of illness or starvation than did. Sheriff Wallar was proud to be the law enforcement officer for the good God-fearing folks of Nevada.

Upon arriving at Tent, he jumped off his horse and shoved his way through the upset crowd. He could not believe what he saw. There, on the ground where they had laid her, was Amanda Buller, bleeding badly.

Though her poor parents had emigrated from England, Amanda, like her younger brother, Gregory, had been born in Illinois. Tent Town was all she knew.

She was a beautiful fifteen year-old that most of the town knew. With a heart of gold, she would help anyone in need. Amanda was special and everyone knew it.

At one time or another, Amanda would have knocked on the door of each Nevada resident and, with a smile as sweet as molasses, sold them some fresh produce her mom and dad had picked that morning.

There wasn't a person who didn't feel the room light up when Amanda walked in. Well, the sheriff could now see there must be one out there who didn't feel that way.

Questioning her brother, Gregory, he said, "So you saw her walking into the woods?"

"Yes, sir, she looked real happy, she did." Gregory had tears flowing down his cheeks and the sheriff wanted so badly to hold the twelve-year-old to make the hurt go away.

"She said this was going to be the best day of her life. That's what she said as she walked off." Gregory was distraught, but trying to hold it together.

Gregory told him Amanda had been seeing Charles Tuxhorn for about three months. Wallar's stomach turned over when he heard the name. He almost wanted to cry himself.

"She didn't say who she was going to see. I just assumed it would be Charles."

"Well, *I* knew it!" Standing behind Gregory, her father switched between shock, pain, and anger. Right now he was feeling the anger. "She told me she finished her chores early so she could have more time to spend with *her* Charles. That's who she went to meet in the woods. Charles Tuxhorn. You gotta go get that butcher, Sheriff!"

Oh, the sheriff planned to do just that. Charles was going to pay for this atrocity, and pay big time. Finally.

Beautiful Amanda. Her long black hair and green eyes were set off by a peaches and cream completion. A lovelier girl could not be found. The sheriff couldn't imagine even a devil like Tuxhorn could hurt her.

Both the father and Gregory told the sheriff they watched her walk into the woods behind the old Miller tent across the way, her long hair flowing in the soft breeze.

"She was beautiful, even from a distance," her father choked, now fighting the pain more than anything else.

"It wasn't more than ten minutes later when we heard the screams. Piercing screams, coming from the woods," he said. "Gregory yelled for me."

It was Amanda and she was screaming for help. They had no idea what in the world could be going on. They both started running toward the sound. Within minutes they found her, almost beaten to death, lying in her own blood at the base of a tree. Near her body was a bloody piece of tree branch. The once-beautiful child was hardly recognizable.

Even filled with so much pain, Gregory returned to his current chore of cutting firewood for the following week.

Sheriff Wallar knew in his heart it was more for releasing his rage at his sister's attack than the need to finish the job.

He was only twelve, but tall for his age. Wallar had heard he wanted to become a preacher when he grew up. His parents had taught him well and he wanted to spread the Gospel of Jesus Christ and Him Crucified for our sins, to others.

The town of Nevada was just as horrified as Tent. Who would want to hurt this beautiful young child? Both communities rallied around to help the family with whatever was needed to doctor this poor child back to health and to get the family through this tragedy.

Amanda was barely alive, and in a coma. Doc Steffens made room for her in his own home so he and his wife could keep a constant eye on her. She wasn't going to get better living out in Tent, so her parents agreed.

Her face and neck were bandaged and the broken arm was wrapped onto boards to keep it straight. A broken ankle was wrapped in cloth and bandaged. It seemed the bruises were everywhere, but the worst injuries were to her head.

The sheriff rode out to Amos Walters' place to question Charles. As he expected, the lying piece-of-crap stated he was doing his chores on the farm at that time. Two other farm workers swore to it, saving Charles from being arrested on the spot.

It made Wallar sick, but until Amanda woke up and told him who her attacker was, there was nothing more he could do. He would take her word over Charles' any day.

He hated the arrogant Tuxhorn. He was sure Amanda would tell them it was Charles who beat her. A new courthouse and jail had been built that very year in Nevada and he was itching to give Charles a really personal tour.

"Here you go, Tuxhorn, your very own cell. May you rot here."

Okay, calm down. Calm down! Sheriff Wallar forced himself to get back to work. His chance at Charles would come later and he was looking forward to it. This time, even the devil couldn't save him from going to prison.

Round-the-clock care and the prayers of the community worked. Amanda did live and awaken from her coma after eighteen days. The sheriff rushed over to the doc's house as soon as he heard. Amanda's parents were there, too.

Doc Steffens said the upgrade of her condition wouldn't help in finding her attacker, because she had no memory whatsoever of what happened that day.

"Her memory of what happened may or may not return. It's probably just as well she doesn't have to relive that horrible time," the doctor said.

Wallar listened as doc further explained her condition. With the broken nose and scars forming on her face, it was also obvious she would never be beautiful again, but no one spoke of that. At least she was alive. Doc also provided medical information which might prove useful later.

~~~

In was summer and Charles felt, at his age of twenty-three, that he should have his own place. He wasn't going to grow old working for someone else and have nothing to show for it.

He wanted to be out on his own. As good a farmer as he was, there wasn't any more Amos Walters could teach him. He was now better at most things than Amos, anyway. All he needed was some nice land and it didn't take him long to find it.

Joseph E. Harding and his wife, Kate, lived in the town of Nevada with their small children—a son and three daughters, one still an infant. At thirty-two, he was a cashier at the bank when he inherited a farm of about eighty-seven acres. They put it up for sale at the going rate of ten dollars an acre. Now they just needed a buyer.

Charles had talked to them about the farm on a couple of occasions. They apparently saw how badly he wanted the land because they agreed to sell it to him for an even $800. It was an excellent price, but still it was more than the savings he had from all his years of slaving for someone else.

Charles was frustrated and angry at another lousy turn in his life. The frustration was taken out on everyone around him. He knew his bad attitude didn't go unnoticed by anyone, but it seemed to be of particular interest to one man.

Charles knew of Whitworth, of course, from almost ten years of living in this area.

William Whitworth was a man of moderate means, providing well, but not extravagantly, for his family. His wife, Bartha, had given him six children, all the way from nineteen years down to five months old. Four of them sons, who would be a big help with on his farm. A daughter, Lillie, was only twelve.

His oldest was a nineteen-year-old girl, Evalee. Eva, as she was called, was still at home and there was not a suitor in sight. Charles knew why that happened to be. She was not much to look at, that was for sure. Compared to his striking good looks, Eva was as plain as they came. What man would want her?

Well, William just walked up to him one day and offered him one thousand dollars to marry Eva. At first, Charles was outraged. A plain dog like that? He'd rather marry a pig. However, after a couple of weeks, that farm was more and more in his thoughts.

As the owners continued to show it to prospective buyers, Charles became afraid someone else would take it away from him. He finally told William he would do it, but he wanted to buy the farm and get it ready before getting married. William found no problem with that and gave him the money.

On the thirty-first day of July, 1880, Charles bought the farm from Joseph Harding for $800 cash. Things were now looking up. With the money he had left and all he had saved from working for Amos, he bought good farming equipment, as well as horses and cows.

He hired some of his friends who had worked at Amos' place. It left Amos painfully short of help, but that was not Charles' concern. He had his own place now and went about building his new house.

One of the contractors Charles hired was Joel Downey, a stone mason. It was said he was the best and that was what Charles wanted. His home was not going to be a pinned together prairie cabin. It would be a substantial two-story structure with the exterior of the first floor in stone.

Joel even added stone to the porch columns. It was not large, but was a mighty fine place nonetheless. Exactly what

Charles felt he deserved. After four months, he moved into the new home and had the old farmhouse torn down.

As Mr. Whitworth watched the fine house being built, he kept asking when Charles was going to marry Eva. For Charles, the answer was always the same—when he had everything ready for her.

But the truth was, Charles was dragging his feet, not wanting to have anything to do with her. Oh, he had gone through some motions by going to spend an evening with the Whitworth family over dinner now and then, showing only his sweet and charming side to Eva and her mother, Bartha.

Charles noticed William seemed quite proud of himself for having acquired a husband for his daughter. It made Charles livid to think he was being treated like a bought and paid-for commodity.

He knew his charms would work on Eva. It was obvious she wasn't used to the attention. Throughout the winter, Charles continued making excuses to Whitworth until early February, 1881, when the unexpected happened once again.

Charles was dumbfounded, but, apparently so was everyone else. The news exploded through Vernon County like wildfire. It was not the kind of news that would hit the front page of the paper. Quite the opposite. It was the kind of news that wasn't even spoken in polite company, but it was big news all the same.

It was the continuation of a tragic story they had all heard before. The young Tent girl, Amanda, who had survived a deadly beating and life-threatening coma, had given birth to a baby boy.

She named him John. John Charles Tuxhorn.

CHAPTER FOURTEEN

It was about a week after the shocking news that Charles was once again visited by Sheriff Wallar. He was coming out of the barn as the sheriff rode up through the melting patches of a week-old snowfall.

The sheriff swung off his horse and walked right up to Charles and leaned into his face. Charles glared back, but knew this was not going to be good.

"Boy, I am going to say it once and only once. I know you beat that girl near to death 'cause she was carrying your child. I know it as well as I'm standing here. And we both know I can't prove it, 'cause she says she don't remember." The sheriff paused for a few seconds, spitting on the ground.

"But I am here to tell you, if you ever attempt to even *see* Amanda or her baby, I will forget I am the law and will hunt you down and kill you, Tuxhorn. And I won't be looking to put a bullet in your sorry heart, either. I will make sure you die slow and painful like. You understand me, *boy?*"

Sheriff Wallar remembered all too well the horrific beating Amanda took and the weeks of fighting not only for her own life, but that of her unborn child. He was not going to let Charles have another chance at either one of them.

"Why would I even *want* to see them, Sheriff?" The only way Charles could get past the accusing eye of the sheriff was to agree with him.

"Ain't my kid, I'm telling you, Sheriff. But I can't stop her naming it what she wants."

Charles was being as nice as he knew how. He knew Sheriff Wallar wanted to kill him where he stood. Charles never ran from a fight, but he would have to be pretty stupid to start one he might not win. This lawman was about to go off the deep end, right in front of him.

"Not one time, Charles. I mean it. I will kill you if you come within fifty feet of anyone in that family. Now, or ten years from now. I will be watching you; don't think I won't." The sheriff spat again, got on his horse, and left the farm. Besides the spit, he also left quite an impression.

At first, Charles could hardly breathe. It was several minutes before his heart was back to beating a normal pattern. There was no doubt in his mind the sheriff meant what he said. Charles was livid Amanda lived at all, let alone her brat. But he had no legal bonds to any of them, so good riddance. But she had the gall to give him the Tuxhorn name. He would deny that bastard child as long as he lived. And who was to say he wouldn't meet up with that kid in a dark alley one night in the years to come, or maybe one of his friends could take care of it. A person couldn't live forever, right?

Charles was relieved when the sheriff rode away. Now, maybe, he could get back to his life. He knew the whole county was aware of Amanda and her child. One of his hired hands had told him some of the things people said about him. It was a good thing he didn't care what any of them thought.

Two days later, Charles stood on his porch at about noon, enjoying a cup of coffee in the cold air. In the winter, a farmer could usually be found pretty close to home. That was where William Whitworth found him. Like everyone else, he had heard about the baby named John Charles Tuxhorn.

"That's it, Charles. No more messing around with your floozies. You and Eva will get married or I want my money back." Whitworth rode right up to the porch and was sitting on his horse as he spoke. Charles knew he was serious.

It was more than a threat. Charles had poured everything he had into his place, to say nothing of his own time and labor. His entire life would be gone. This was *his* farm!

"I will be expecting you for dinner this evening…a very *special* dinner, right?" Whitworth's eyes were squinting, but he managed a half smile. He tipped his hat and rode away. Charles felt blindsided, in a trap he couldn't get out of.

As soon as he was out of sight, Charles let go of his pent-up rage in a frightening tantrum that scared the hands coming out of the barn into running back inside. They knew better than to cross Tuxhorn. His violent temper was well known, and it was pretty obvious he wasn't having a good day.

"That dirt-sucking swine can take my farm away from me if he wants to and he will if I don't marry that cow." Anger and rage filled him.

He danced around on one foot as he pulled off a boot and threw it. His voice became shrill and loud. Charles was throwing a physical and mental temper tantrum and was out of control. His fists were swinging at the air, feet kicking at nothing, and mouth swearing. Anything he could kick at or throw at or yell at, or, better yet...

The thought of killing the whole Whitworth family stopped his tirade. He stood perfectly still in his yard, contemplating this new thought. *If they were all dead, this Eva problem would be solved. He would be free to live his life as he wanted to.* There would be no one left to force him into anything. There would be no one demanding their money back. It made a lot of sense. Ugly scenarios flashed through his raging mind. *How about a house fire...too bad everyone was home...*He almost smiled at the thought.

Then he realized the problem with that scenario. Getting rid of the Whitworths would solve one problem, but on the heels of this Amanda thing, he would be caught for sure. That slimy sheriff would be watching him all the time now. Getting rid of two women, back to back, might not be such a good idea.

Rage returned when he realized he was going to have to go along with it for now. He might be forced into a marriage, but he couldn't be forced to love her. *Love her?* He felt nothing but contempt for her and her whole stupid family.

It was about seven that evening, after supper at the Whitworths', when Charles asked Eva to go walking with him. Outside, without much fanfare, he asked Eva if she would be his wife. She smiled sweetly and accepted.

On March 2, 1881, barely a month after the birth of John, Charles married Evalee Whitworth. And he hated her for it. This was no different than the trap his witch of a mother had done to his father. For the first time, Charles figured it wasn't too surprising his old man hated everyone, because right now, he did, too.

From the beginning, he made her life miserable. He was abusive and beat her without cause. Charles knew she had nowhere to turn. Her father wouldn't interfere; he wouldn't dare. She was his now and he could do what he wanted with her.

Eva couldn't do anything right and nothing would change his hatred of her. The house was never clean enough. The food was never good enough. He made sure Eva knew there was no love in him for her. Or anyone, for that matter.

Then the inevitable happened. He found out his wife was pregnant. If he thought there could be nothing worse than being married to her, he was wrong. Having to raise her brat definitely made it worse. He hated the thought of having a kid around. He didn't want any, let alone the ugly ones he felt she would have.

On the heels of Amanda, Charles knew he couldn't try to get rid of her kid, too. He now had to accept he was to be a family man, but he didn't have to like it. That brat had better stay out of his way.

On September 16, 1882, she gave birth to a baby girl she named Bertha Mae. He immediately berated her for having a girl. It proved she was worthless. Boys were the only thing that counted. He wanted farm help, not another whiny weakling like her.

The following year, in 1883, Eva gave birth to a son, Edward. Charles wasn't quite so upset, but by the time Edward could walk, Charles enjoyed slapping him across the room just to hear him cry.

It actually pleased him to be mean to the children. He didn't want them to feel too loved in this world. No one loved him and they weren't going to be spoiled by it, either. Showing them the real side of life was his job, wasn't it?

~~~

Eva put Bertha and Edward in a small room by themselves when their father came home. She figured if he couldn't see them, maybe he wouldn't think about them. If he didn't think about them, maybe he wouldn't want to hurt them. Keeping her children out of harm's way was always on her mind.

"Bertha, you stay in here with your brother and don't come out and bother your daddy. Okay?" Eva knew she was too young to understand, but somewhere in her tiny mind, Bertha seemed to know it was for the best.

At only two years old, it was obvious Bertha was going to look more like her mother than anyone else. She was very cute, but in a plain way. Eva loved her son, Edward, with all her heart, but maybe it was the fact that Bertha was the firstborn, because she loved her little girl more than life itself.

They all did whatever it took to stay out of Charles' way. But even Eva wasn't prepared for the turmoil that came from out of state. She knew it would send him into a rage.

It was in the fall of 1884—November, to be exact—when news came from McPherson County, Kansas. From what she heard in town, there were newspaper headlines that went from the east coast to the west coast of America.

Every major newspaper, and many minor ones, ran the story. The Tuxhorns were a household name. Even knowing how depraved Charles was, Eva was still shocked to hear the news.

August Tuxhorn tried to burn his entire family alive, before he committed suicide.

CHAPTER FIFTEEN

November was a terrible time for a funeral. It was far too chilly; at least Elizabeth Tuxhorn thought so. It was no time to be outside, but here she was. They all were. She sat in front, with many of her children sitting behind her. Lewis, her eighteen-year-old son, sat beside her and held one of her trembling hands. Leo Lewis. What would she ever do without the dear boy?

It turned out to be very cold, that winter morning in 1884, but then again, what November morning wasn't? She was having a hard time concentrating on what was going on. The doctor had given her some powders to calm her nerves. He told her they were powerful and would help her get through the funeral. Maybe that was why she didn't seem to care what was going on around her. Silly thoughts even entered her head and that certainly wasn't proper.

There was the Catholic priest ready to preside over her husband's funeral. They didn't go to the Catholic Church. She and the children were members of the Methodist Church.

August would rather die than step into a church. *Gee, seems that's what he did.* Elizabeth almost giggled out loud and was horrified at her thoughts.

Their Methodist pastor had taken ill the week before and wasn't back on his feet yet. Elizabeth had asked the priest if he would do it and was told he would, if he could conduct it in the proper Catholic manner. Elizabeth could have cared less how he conducted it, as long as it got done. *Don't be snippy, Elizabeth. This is not the time to be childish.*

Friends from all over the county were here to pay their respects. Not for August, certainly. They didn't have any respect for her violent, mean husband. However, she had remained the prim and proper wife over the eight years or so that they had lived there.

She pulled her black coat tighter around her. The cold wind was seeping into her bones. As she pulled, the collar got caught on something under it. Elizabeth automatically reached inside and adjusted the large cameo brooch, made of mother-of-pearl, she was wearing on her long black dress. The brooch was one of the few things that survived the fire. When she touched it, she thought about the chain. It used to have a chain that made it a necklace, but she hadn't been able to find it in years. It must have gotten lost in the move from Illinois.

It was back in '76 when they moved from Illinois. August wanted a change, and she didn't care anymore. Her brother, Anton, had never spoken to her again after her marriage to August. She had learned to accept that, in his eyes, she was a fallen woman.

Her two oldest sons—William, then nineteen, and Edward, seventeen—wanted to stay in Illinois and make it on their own. She gave her blessing. She felt they were ready.

Well, that is not exactly the truth, now is it, Elizabeth? Liar, liar! William is not your oldest son, is he? It's Charles! That was one person she had no use for, that Charles. He would now be twenty-eight-years-old, or so. Elizabeth had neither seen nor heard from him since August sent him away at the age of fourteen. But she had certainly heard *about* him. Rumors raced back to Illinois that he was in Missouri and had a bastard son named John. *Figures. Good news travels fast; bad news travels faster; doesn't it, Elizabeth? He has been humiliating you since before he was born. Would it ever stop?* As if she needed any more gossip about her. She had no use for the likes of him or any kid of his.

Mean and crazy like his father, Charles was. There was no way she could have two of them in the same house. Oh, some of her children had anger problems, but they were teachable. Some were sweet as fresh buttermilk. But that Charles was a lost cause. Pure hate lived in those blue eyes of his. And he was dangerous, just like his father.

His father. What a joke. August hated all of his children. He never was a father to any of them. He was a crazy, violent, fat old drunk. *Yes,* Elizabeth thought, *that about summed it up.*

The fact was, she knew August had been getting much worse over the past few years. How many times had she caught him talking to himself, just like he was carrying on a conversation with an invisible person? She shuddered as she thought about the times she heard him yelling and arguing at nothing.

His wild blue eyes would be cloudy, looking almost gray. No one was with him, but he would curse, swinging his arms and kicking with his feet like he was talking to the devil himself. *Wonder if the devil was afraid of my husband? Now, calm down, Elizabeth, you have a funeral to get through.*

It was before they left Illinois that she put a stop to bearing any more children. She decided there would be no more babies for him to hate. Her tenth child was born back in '75 and she told herself ten was a respectable number for any woman, and there didn't need to be any more.

One day when August came home, all of his things had been moved into a bedroom in the back of the house. That drunken dog would never touch her again. Sure, he was mad—furious in fact—but she didn't care. He tried to beat her, but he had gained weight with age and couldn't push her around much anymore. She took an old skillet and let him have it right over the top of his thick head. She didn't see him for two days. As she recalled, *they were two really good days.*

Selling out in Illinois had been easy. The only nice thing she could ever say about August was that he was rich. Not like a king, exactly, but wealthy enough that she could live well and have almost everything she wanted; as long as she didn't tell her husband about it.

Their home in Kansas was lovely, sitting on 240 acres of prime farmland. She had the house fixed up just as any proper home should be. Elizabeth choked on her thoughts. Everything was gone now. Not a stick survived. Of course, that was exactly what August wanted. *Not to fear, dead husband. The next house will be much nicer – especially with you not being in it...*

August is dead and he went out with a bang! Oh for heaven's sake, Elizabeth, straighten up. That was highly improper. What will people think? Well, at least she didn't say it out loud. She glanced around just to make sure.

She knew, without a doubt, it was the powders making her think such vile things. She would never have had that thought on her own. Never.

As expected, the priest proceeded with the primary service in Latin.

Hoc autem dico fratres quoniam caro et sanguis regnum Dei possidere non possunt neque corruptio incorruptelam possidebit...

But he did, she thought. *Go out with a bang, that is.* The memories of that day were still raw. *Only, what? Three...four days ago?* She couldn't remember. It seemed like another lifetime. So much had changed.

August was on just another one of his drunken benders. He had spent more and more time sleeping in the barn, instead of the house, the past few months. That was fine with her. She hated him being in the house when he was drinking. He made everyone miserable. It seemed that was his purpose in life, trying to make everyone around him as miserable as he was.

...ecce mysterium vobis dico omnes quidem resurgemus sed non omnes inmutabimur...

The children were already in bed asleep. She had just gotten into her nightgown when she heard the noise. What a noise it was. It sounded like the front door just burst open. *But,* when she thought about it, *that was exactly what happened.* *BANG!*

She ran out of her room to the stop of the stairs and there was her husband. The man was drunk as a skunk and raving like a demon. With age, he had become as round as he was tall, which would have made him look amusing except for the shotgun he was waving around. If it wasn't for the wall he was leaning on, he probably wouldn't have been able to stand.

"Get your drunken butt back out in the barn. Only decent folks sleep here!" Boy, was she furious. She was sick to death with his ways. Sick to death for her children, as much as for herself.

"Get...here...wo...! You ca...can't...tal me tha...ay!" August was stumbling over himself, as well as his words.

"Had it...wiff...gon kill...you...all...you." With those words, she saw him start up the stairs. It became obvious he wanted to begin with her. Trying to steady himself, he started to point his shotgun up at her.

There was no way Elizabeth was going to watch while he killed her, or her family. She quickly jumped down a couple of stairs until he was closer to her. Bracing herself on the stairway walls, she lifted one foot up to his chest and shoved him backward. And backward down the stairs he went.

...in momento in ictu oculi in novissima tuba canet enim et mortui resurgent incorrupti et nos inmutabimur.

Elizabeth looked up at the priest, who appeared to be in his own Latin world. *Wouldn't it be funny if the priest didn't even know what he was saying? No, it wouldn't be funny, Elizabeth!* Ashamed at her thoughts, she forced herself to look away.

Her thoughts quickly returned to that night. Lord, he did land with a crash at the bottom of those stairs. The moaning told her he was still alive, saved, no doubt, by the alcohol. He continued to moan as he rolled over on his knees to get up. Finally standing, he picked up his shotgun from the floor and went out the door yelling he would be back.

> *Oportet enim corruptibile hoc induere incorruptelam et mortale hoc induere inmortalitatem; cum autem mortal...*

Elizabeth believed him. She had lived with that despicable man for twenty-eight long years and knew he was crazy enough to make good on his threat. She had to do something, and do it quickly.

Running back up the stairs, she started yelling for all of the children.

"Wake up! Everyone! Get up! We have to leave right now! Get up!" She knew her time was limited. She opened each door and yelled some more.

"No time to take anything, run, let's go!" She was in near panic mode by this time.

Her children came out of their rooms rubbing their eyes and half frightened to death. She didn't blame them a bit. Her heart was flipping over, too.

"Go out the back door. Go! *Not* the front. Hear me? You *must* leave by the back door. Move!" There wasn't time to answer questions; they had to mind her immediately.

Elizabeth's mind was in sharp alert as she counted heads going out the back. After getting everyone out of the house, they ran for the wooded area near the front road. Elizabeth had everyone sit down on the ground in the trees so they couldn't be seen. She did the same and held a couple of the youngest ones. Lewis had his arms around the older ones. The ground was cold and damp, but no one was going to complain.

"Quiet, children. Not one word out of your mouths. Our lives depend on it." She hated scaring the children further than they already were, but there was no other way to indicate the danger they were in. Luckily they seemed to sense the threat was real and they were too petrified to make a sound.

> ...*hoc induerit inmortalitatem tunc fiet sermo qui scriptus est absorta est mors in victoria ubi est mors victoria tua ubi est mors stimulus tuus.*

They hadn't been seated on the cold ground more than a minute when they saw August come stumbling out of the barn with a burning torch. A quiet but collective gasp could be heard among them as they watched the horror in front of them.

August walked up to the front of the house and yelled to the family he thought was inside.

"If I can't sho...shooo...will...burn...had...it...wif..."
He then used the torch to set the house on fire, starting
with the front door. Covering the front area first, he didn't
stop there. He kept talking nonsense that they couldn't
understand as he walked around each side of the house and
set it on fire as he went. It became a massive inferno within
minutes, right before their eyes.

Elizabeth knew he was drunk, but he still had brains
enough to make sure there would be no escape route. All four
sides were burning, including the doors. Part of her didn't
believe he was as drunk as he seemed, because his actions
were just too well calculated to achieve his goal. But, in light
of all this, what did she know about anything anymore?

She remembered her heart had been in her throat as she
watched. *He really was going to kill us all. If he had his way, he
would have burned us to death!*

Now, sitting here at the funeral, the memories of that
night made Elizabeth's hands start shaking again. Lewis
reached over and held them both this time. She looked over
at him with a weak smile. She could see the pain in her boy's
eyes, too. What it must have been like for the children to
watch their father try to murder them. But watch they did;
they had no choice.

She couldn't remember how long they watched the fire
burn. Of course, it seemed like hours, but she knew in her
heart it was probably just minutes. The house was a blazing
inferno. Even at the tree line where they were hiding, they
could feel the treacherous heat. There would be little, if
anything, she could save.

Stimulus autem mortis peccatum est virtus vero peccati lex Deo autem gratias qui dedit nobis victoriam per Dominum nostrum Iesum Christum.

The priest was pouring out his best Latin while her eyes wandered. She saw many friends and neighbors barely paying any attention to the requiem. She couldn't blame them—who knew what he was even saying? *August sure didn't.*

Funerals were for the living, anyway. They were never for the dead. She figured if you liked the dead person, you went to a funeral to say goodbye. If you didn't like them, well, you went to make sure they were really dead. That pretty much summed up how she felt. *Just making sure you're really dead, husband dear!*

Are you there, August, in your little wooden box? Elizabeth thought for a moment she was going to be physically ill. These crazy thoughts were annoying, to say the least.

Was it really less than a week ago? Nothing was clear to her any more. *It's got to be the powder.* She won't be taking that again. *A woman needs her wits about her to stay alive in this world.*

She remembered their clothes were damp and cold as they sat on the ground watching their home burn up into nothing.

That's when it happened. As if nothing worse could be imagined, August wasn't finished yet.

He walked back into the barn and set it on fire. They watched as they could see the flames licking the outside of the door frame. The screams of the horses about did the children in. A couple of the younger ones started to cry. At this point, Elizabeth didn't try to stop them. She was about on the verge herself. Who could be so cruel, they would burn horses alive? *Well, silly, the same vile man who would burn his family alive...*

They watched as he exited the burning barn and appeared to be looking for something. He was ranting and yelling about something. None of his words made any sense to her. He found a tree stump and sat himself down.

What happened next took a total of about one minute, but it would forever seem to her to be an eternity.

Elizabeth would never forget. She was quite sure her children wouldn't, either.

August tied something to his shotgun. She couldn't tell what it was, at first. He positioned himself on the edge of the stump, took his shotgun, and put the barrel under his chin. He took the string he had obviously tied to the trigger and pulled.

They watched him blow his head off. That was it. Nothing more.

Mother and children sat in silence, staring at the horror in front of them. Their home was burning to the ground. The barn, with their beloved horses, was burning as well.

Then, their father became a fragment of a human being. Their world had become hell on earth. There was no other way for Elizabeth to describe it. With all the heat and flames, it had to be what hell looked like. She reminded herself to be more punctual with her prayers from now on.

Even tears wouldn't come now. Maybe it wasn't real. Maybe they would wake up from this nightmare. Maybe...

The fire had roused many of the neighbors and they were on their way to help, but there wasn't anything they could do when they arrived. Elizabeth saw they rode onto the farm slowly, as if unsure whether they wanted to be there. But August, or what was left of him, was easy to find. No longer feeling a threat from him, they now scattered, quickly trying to find the rest of the family, appearing to fear the worst.

They immediately surrounded the house, trying to see if there were any survivors. Elizabeth could hear their comments. They thought the whole family was dead.

It was a while before someone found the family sitting in the trees. They had not moved nor said a word. They just stared. It wasn't out of fear, or even dread. Just the horrifying scene that each of them were witnessing. She now knew they were all in shock, but at that point, nothing mattered. They were each helped out of the trees by caring neighbors, but she couldn't tell who they were. She didn't know who she was...

Elizabeth was grateful for their kindness that night. They helped each one up off the ground and helped them all get over to Fred Weigand's place. Fred said they could stay with him and the missus until their new house was built. The community would see they all had clothes by tomorrow.

A wonderful, kind man, that Weigand, and his wife had been a life saver this week. Good people, that's for sure. The whole community was.

In the name of the Father, the Son and the Holy Spirit, Amen.

DONALIE BELTRAN

Lewis was shaking her shoulder.

"Mother, it's over. We have to go."

Elizabeth's mind snapped back to the present. People were beginning to wander away from the funeral. Lewis helped her stand, but she wanted to stay for a few more minutes. She knew her son was watching her with concern, as the workmen placed the casket in the ground and started to refill the hole with earth.

As they were shovelling dirt, she walked up close, removed the brooch inside her coat, and threw in onto the wooden box below, as the dirt continued to cover it for eternity. *I will hate you forever for not being the man I fell in love with.* Somehow, Elizabeth knew, it was finally over.

As her son helped her walk away from her husband's grave, Elizabeth couldn't help but think, *at the age of fifty-three, August's time on this earth is over.*

But hers wasn't. Now she and the children could live without the terror and shame he brought to their lives. The thought made her smile.

All in all, Elizabeth felt it had been a good day.

~~~

The newspaper people were mesmerized with the story from coast to coast. Telegraphs sent the horror, like wildfire. Elizabeth and the children had lived through enough headlines already, but she knew there would be more.

Farmer Tries To Kill Family, Then Self. – McPherson, Kansas

155

A Demented Farmer - Destroys His Property And Takes His Own Life – Philadelphia Inquirer

A Violent Suicide – Rocky Mountain News

Self Murder Of A Kansas Incendiary"– Muskegon Chronicle, Michigan Fired His House And Blew His Brains Out! – Salt Lake Tribune, Utah

The New York Times wrote:

A FARMER'S INSANE ACT –

McPherson County, Kansas, November 13, 1884. August Tuxhorn, a farmer of this county, today set fire to his house, barn and granary, and then blew his brains out with a shotgun, all in a drunken rage.

The buildings were destroyed, together with $4,000 in money, which was in the house: total loss, $11,000. Evidence showed that he entered the house with the intent to murder his wife and the four children in the home but his wife kicked him back down the stairs at which time he left.

She got all the children out of the house before he came back and torched it. No cause is assigned to his act except that he was a man of great temper.

It is said his father killed himself some years back."

CHAPTER SIXTEEN

Charles had no contact with his parents for the past fourteen years, nor did he want any now. It was a surprise to him when he learned they had moved to Kansas. The problem was, everyone else in the United States knew it at the same time he did.

The front page of the newspapers screamed out the story of how August killed himself after burning up his house and barn, thinking he had burned his family alive. He also killed some horses, it seemed. *Leave it up to his old man to set the news on fire, too.* He chuckled at his clever thought. It was, however, the only thing he thought was funny.

The story was teletyped to newspapers across the country. Presses were held up while the latest was being readied for the next edition. They just couldn't get enough of the man who died in such a violent manner, one who would burn his family alive. Unfortunately, that included the newspaper in Vernon County, Missouri.

It took a lot to stop Charles in his tracks, but that certainly did. No matter where he went, everyone knew the story. His father was a crazy, drunken, murderer.

No one dared mention it to him, but talk among themselves spread like a cold winter wind. With the news of the violence in his family, everyone now knew he took after his old man. Behind his back, he knew they were saying he was crazy, too. To be compared to August was the one thing Charles could not tolerate.

One day in town, a man snickered as he walked by Charles. The insinuation was all he could stand and the fight was on. It took four men to pull him off the poor man, but his point was made. He wouldn't tolerate disrespect. The man managed to live, and didn't press charges. Charles was pretty sure he wouldn't, if he wanted to stay alive.

He was livid his father had invaded his life again. Even in death, the old man haunted him. What did it take to get that man out of his life forever?

He knew it would be years, if ever, before he would get over this latest humiliation. He could feel the rage in his heart threatening to explode. Charles hated most people, but he hated being out of control of his own life more.

How many times had he heard about what an idiot his grandfather was for being a drunk and committing suicide? August spoke Henry's name with such hatred. Nonetheless, he repeated those actions and destroyed everything around him to boot. How could he do that? *Only a fool would do such a thing!* He never wanted to hear the man's name again.

Charles never spoke about his parents to anyone. He hadn't since the day he left Illinois. They were both dead to him. At least, until August decided to be dead again and make headline news. No, he didn't think that was funny at all.

~~~

Eva's family never came over any more. They were afraid to. Nor were Charles and Eva Tuxhorn invited to the Whitworth farm. No one knew what Charles would do next. His violence was out of control, and no one wanted to be around him when it happened.

They now knew what kind of man he truly was, and William stopped trying to make excuses for him. Eva knew her father would never forgive himself for putting his own daughter into such harm, but who in the world could have known the man was a dangerous psychopath? She surely didn't.

At times, when Charles was in town or across the county buying livestock, Eva would slip over to her parents' house to visit. The times were short and far between, but it was the only happiness she knew.

Eva knew her father was afraid of Charles. Now that they were married, her father could no longer hold the farm over Tuxhorn's head. Oh, she knew all about the money to buy the farm. She wasn't stupid and it was easy to figure out. She knew a plain girl like herself was not going to be the pick of the best-looking man in the county without some compensation. She knew that. She just didn't know the man her father picked for her was insane.

As her father got older, his physical fear of her husband was very real to him. But then again, who wasn't afraid of Charles Tuxhorn? Nobody dared to cross him.

After the news about August Tuxhorn—his murder attempts and suicide—Charles was worse than ever. It was almost as if he was in a contest with his dead father to see who could be the most evil. Eva never knew August, but she was surely betting on Charles to win.

She didn't have any more children after Edward until 1890, when Mary Ethel was born. Blaine was born in 1892, followed by Matilda in 1893.

Charles' wrath did not cease toward her, the children, or the world for that matter. He seemed to be out to prove something, but no one knew what it was. Eva had long ago known her destiny was set, but the lives of her children were the most important to her. It was a miracle her children lived through the tyranny, but she did everything she could to keep them safe and show them her love.

Louis was born in 1896 and Amos in 1899. These babies needed her to survive. She shivered to think what their world would be like if they didn't have her.

The farm flourished and the years seemed to be copies of the ones before them. Eva had seven children, all of whom knew the wrath of a father who hated them. His womanizing never stopped, but Eva was actually grateful for any evening he wasn't at home terrorizing her or the children.

Over the years, he spent more time in the barn than in the house. She saw many nice things delivered out there, but she didn't care about anything but her own little world with her children.

Each year, however, it seemed she would bear a new scar on her face or arms. Charles liked clubbing or cutting, almost as much as punching her and the children in the stomach. Somewhere along the line, she stopped feeling pain. When she saw it coming, her mind switched off and she usually couldn't remember what happened next. Before she knew it, she was left alone to clean up the mess, or the blood, or both.

In the year 1900, Eva once again found herself pregnant. Another baby to shield from Charles wasn't what she needed, but that was no longer her choice. She was going to have her eighth child.

~~~

Charles came home one evening in a rage. Some floozy had told him to get his hands off her and "go home" to his wife and kids. Though still good-looking, in his mid-forties he was no longer the number one choice of the young women of the day. He was angry and was going to take it out on someone. Or a bunch of *little* someones.

When he came through the door, the children didn't have time to scatter. The first one he saw was seven-year-old Matilda. He grabbed her and threw her against the wall.

He picked up four-year-old Louis and that was when Eva stepped in. It was something she had never done before.

She grabbed the little boy from his arms and screamed at him to leave her babies alone. For one moment in her life, *she* was the one out of control.

"I am sick of you hurting these children for no reason! Leave them alone. Leave me alone! Leave us all alone!" She was screaming and crying at the same time. No one had ever heard her raise her voice to anyone, let alone scream at her violent husband. She had been pushed to the edge and was quickly falling over it.

Charles had stopped in motion, as did all the children. They were staring at their momma as if she was a stranger. No one knew she had much of a voice, let alone a loud one. Charles stared at her.

"I won't let you hurt them anymore. It's over! You get out of here and don't come back. I know my daddy's money bought this farm. You think I am stupid? I can get the sheriff to make you leave!" Eva had let out twenty years of anguish and pain in a total of two minutes.

She stood in front of him as she was running out of steam. As her voice came back down, her fear returned. She stood there, staring at the devil himself. She felt she was going to die.

To everyone's surprise, Charles never said a word. After staring at her for several minutes, he turned and left, not to return the rest of the night.

The next day, he filed for a divorce.

CHAPTER SEVENTEEN

P laintiff states that on the second day of March, 1881, in Vernon County, Missouri, he was lawfully married to the defendant and continue to live with defendant as her husband from and after said date until the eleventh day of September, 1900;

that during all that time plaintiff faithful demeaned himself and discharged all his duties as the husband of the defendant, and at all times treated her with kindness and affection; but said defendant, wholly disregarding her duties as the wife of the plaintiff, has been guilty of adultery at diverse and sundry times, to-wit:

with one Johnson, during the year 1883; about the year 1895 with one Robert Tront; about the years 1895-6 with one William Crowley and with one Charley Robinson; that defendant has offered to this plaintiff such indignities as to render his condition intolerable, this this, to-wit:

Sometime during the month of October or November 1899, the defendant knocked the plaintiff down with an iron rod; that during July 1900, the defendant struck the plaintiff with a pitchfork, cutting his face with the prongs; that during the month of August, 1900, the defendant threatened to kill the plaintiff and did strike at him with a butcher knife, and called him all kinds of vile and abusive names;

that during said month of August 1900, the defendant threatened to burn the hay and barn of the defendant and threatened to knock her children's brains out; that defendant has abused and mistreated the children born of said marriage.

So said the divorce petition. It was such an outrage that people came for miles to sit in on the case. Sheriff Minshaw had better things to do, but the judge had asked him to stand in the back and keep an eye on things, as he felt they could get out of hand pretty easily. So here he was.

There were five male witnesses against Eva in the divorce trial. All five men said they had "occasion to be with Eva" during her marriage. A pregnant Eva never said a word during the proceedings to defend herself. How could she? The men had all worked for Charles over the past few years. It was her word against all of them.

The sheriff knew, even in 1900, a woman didn't have much credibility. She just stared down at the table in front of her. His heart went out to her. Poor lady. Hadn't she already suffered enough, and with a baby in her and all?

Most of Vernon County knew of the Tuxhorns and that she was an abused wife. The testimony was not true—everyone knew that—but there was nothing that could be done under the law. Half the time, Sheriff Minshaw thought he was going to be sick to his stomach.

He also knew the Vernon County Judge, Chester H. Kinley, was gritting his teeth and burning inside for what he knew was false testimony against an innocent woman. But the judge had to abide by the law. They all did. A man could get a divorce from a woman who cheated, and he had five witnesses to back him up.

Charles even told his phoney pack of witnesses to talk about a birthmark Eva had on her thigh so it sounded like they really saw it for themselves. There, in court, the pain and shame on Eva's face told everyone she couldn't take much more.

It didn't surprise the sheriff, or anyone else, when Charles was granted a divorce in October of 1900. He was awarded the farm and custody of the children. It wasn't often Minshaw had to watch it, but sometimes, just sometimes, justice failed the people. There was no doubt in anyone's mind that this was one of those times.

~~~

"So you thought you were going to throw me out of my own home, did you? Well, looky here, cow, you are the one without a home." Standing in his house, Charles always had the last word. Always.

Near tears, Eva's voice was low and subdued, "What about the children? They need me."

"*Really?* They need you?" Charles took the back of his hand and slapped her across the face. She fell backward onto the floor.

"They *need* you? Well fine, then, I will let you stay. But you are nothing to me but a servant. You will take care of the house and the kids according to my orders. You can live in MY house, on MY farm and take care of MY children, *if* you behave! Any sign of disrespect from you and you're gone, you hear me? You will never see those kids again."

The satisfaction Charles felt was a huge rush. *The witch. Who does she think she is dealing with?*

"Okay, Charles. Okay. You win." Eva's voice was so low he barely made it out.

"I always win, *Eva*. You should have known that by now. Don't ever forget it again." Charles actually smiled as he left the house and walked to the barn to joke around with his hired help.

"Boys! It's time to enjoy the rest of the day. Let's all go to May Belle's and hump some of her girls. The good time is on me!" Charles knew how to repay the guys for lying in court. Plus, he was going to get some good stuff, for a change.

It was indeed a good time in his life. He was legally rid of Eva. He let her stay around to take care of the kids. She wanted to, and, in truth, he needed her to, because he wasn't going to do it himself. Everything belonged to him and only him now. She had no say in anything that went on and she had to live like a hired servant. He had her right where he wanted her. Life was good.

It took a whole lot longer than he had initially planned, but he was finally rid of the entire Whitworth family. Legally, anyway, and he could deal with that for now.

CHAPTER EIGHTEEN

Fred M. Minshaw had been Sheriff of Vernon County now for less than two years. He loved his job and planned on keeping it as long as possible. His old friend, and former sheriff, Frank Wallar, had not forgotten about Charles Tuxhorn and wouldn't let him, either.

Frank was a regular visitor at the Sheriff's Office, sitting on the front porch shooting the bull with all the deputies and Fred. He made sure they all knew about Charles Tuxhorn and his violent ways. They chewed on straw or the occasional cigar and talked about the people walking down the street.

"Don't you boys forget about Charles, now. How he tried to kill that young gal and her baby. Finally caused her death, too," Wallar said. "He's mean and evil as they come and it's real hard to catch him at it. The man gets away with everything, it seems. You keep an eye on that scumbag."

Sheriff Minshaw's comment was always the same. "Frank, there is no need to keep reminding us. We know only too well what a scar on this county he is."

He knew Wallar's intentions were good, but Vernon County didn't need reminding. Everyone knew Tuxhorn was the son of the devil, including the law. What to do about it was another story.

It was one that finally might have a happy ending. A happy ending for some people, anyway.

Sheriff Minshaw was married to the sister of County Court Judge, his Honor Chester H. Kinley, the very one who oversaw the Tuxhorn divorce. It was a close-knit family and they gathered every Sunday after church for dinner at the judge's house. This particular Sunday, Minshaw and the judge went walking while the wives cleaned up after a nice meal.

Lighting cigars, they commented on what a mild autumn it had been so far. The air was crisp and pleasant. Dinner was mighty fine. The women folk had done a good job, no doubt. Minshaw knew something was bothering his brother-in-law, but he wasn't going to push it until Chester was ready to talk.

"There is something I need to talk to you about," the judge said, looking over at Fred with great affection.

"Spit it out, Chester," Fred said, taking another tug on one of his host's fine cigars. He had nothing but love and respect for the judge. A finer man you would never meet. There was only three years difference in the sisters they married, but there was ten years between the sheriff and the judge, Fred being the junior. He looked up to his learned friend with respect.

"I want Charles Tuxhorn out of here. I mean out of the whole County of Vernon; in fact, the whole state of *Missouri!*" The normally mild-mannered judge was getting more agitated by the minute. "I don't care how you do it, Fred, but I want him gone. Whatever it takes!

"He has been a scourge on this county for the past twenty-odd years. And the travesty he just made out of my courtroom will be his last in my jurisdiction." Judge Kinley was seething as he remembered.

Fred knew exactly what he meant. He nodded and said, "You mean all those liars he brought into court?"

"Yes, indeed. I felt so sorry for his poor wife I could barely sit through it all," said the judge. "He spits in the face of the law every time, and I won't put up with it any more. The whole county knows how he beats his family into submission, and now he has taken everything from that poor woman, including her own children."

"Consider it done, Chester. Consider it done." The sheriff was more than happy to carry out his brother-in-law's wishes. Especially this one.

The judge gave him a big smile and said, "Thanks, Fred. It never hurts to have a sheriff in the family."

The next day, on Monday, Sheriff Minshaw sent his deputy to inform Charles he had to appear in the Sheriff's Office no later than Tuesday. When his deputy returned, they had a good laugh at how mad Tuxhorn had gotten.

"Sheriff, you wouldn't believe the look on his face. He demanded to know who 'that sheriff thought he was' ordering him to do *anything*." The deputy was having a hard time to keep from laughing while trying to talk.

"I told him you was the sheriff, that's who. I thought he was going to kill me right there," the deputy said with a chuckle.

"Come on, what did he say next?" Sheriff Minshaw was enjoying this as much as his deputy.

"Well, sir, he said he didn't have to do nothing that he didn't want to. I told him that he had better *want* to come see you, then, because he would be arrested if he didn't show up. I just turned my horse around and rode off. I do believe I could still hear him swearing as I rode by the old church pond."

They both laughed until their sides hurt and the tears came. Some jobs were just more fun than others.

The following day, as ordered, Charles Tuxhorn stomped into the Sheriff's Office, arrogant and demanding to know why he had been so rudely inconvenienced.

"Why am I here instead of working my crops like I'm supposed to be?" Charles yelled, loud enough to wake the dead. It didn't work, though; only the sheriff was present.

Wallar told him to sit down and watched as he reluctantly did so. He then calmly leaned back in his chair, ready to set Tuxhorn's world upside down. He was slowly drawing on a cigar and enjoying every minute of the disgusted look on his visitor's face.

He had to do things in the past to obtain justice for the community, but this time was different. This wasn't just a job, it was personal. Tuxhorn had hurt many people in the county. It was time he was stopped, at least in Minshaw's jurisdiction. What was it the judge said, 'Whatever it took...'

"You are in a whole lot of trouble, Tuxhorn." The sheriff was going to really enjoy this.

"And how is that, Sheriff?" Charles spat out the words, not even trying to hide the disgust he felt for the man sitting across the desk.

"Well, seems you are going to be arrested for lying under oath, paying another party to lie under oath, obtaining a divorce under false pretences—which of course will nullify the divorce. And that means your wife will get the farm *and* the children while you rot in jail, which mea....."

"You are full of *crap*, Sheriff!" Livid, Charles had jumped up from the chair, knocking it backwards across the room, and was leaning over the sheriff's desk. "She never denied *any* of it!"

"Oh, I know she didn't. Scared for her life and that of her kids, I reckon." The sheriff hadn't had this much fun in a long while. And this cigar was really good. *I need to tell the judge how I appreciate his taste in cigars.*

"Thing about it is, one of your so-called witnesses came forward and told the truth!"

Charles' anger was evident all over his face. "Now, which one would that be, Sheriff?" His voice was low, deliberate, and full of sarcasm.

"You know I can't tell you that, Charles. If I did, I doubt he would live 'til morning, and we are going to need him to testify against you. But the fact is, you are still going to go to jail."

"What is it you want, Sheriff?" Charles said.

Minshaw knew Charles was trying to control his hatred for the lawman in front of him, but the rage was evident by his voice.

"I would already be under arrest if you didn't *want* something." Charles almost spit as he talked.

"Well, now, you're right about that, Charles. I don't like it at all, but it seems the county judge wants to give you a solution to your problem. If it was left up to me, your butt would already be enjoying the hospitality of the State of Missouri.

"You have thirty days to leave the county; actually, the state. The end of November is your limit. On December first, I have the authority to arrest your sorry ass, which I must say would be the highlight of my year." The sheriff was having a hard time not to laugh out loud.

"And another thing...if any one of them boys you used as witnesses is killed before you leave, I will see to it you hang for murder. Fact is, deal is off if any of them are even *hurt* before you leave."

"You can't do that, you filthy pig!" Charles was nearing a breaking point.

Now standing, he leaned over into Tuxhorn's face. Sheriff Minshaw lowered his voice into a threatening tone and, never more serious in his life, stated, "Oh, but I can, Tuxhorn and I *will*. End of November. Take it...or *leave* it." He knew he was staring into Satan's blue eyes, but he didn't flinch.

The sheriff could see he had him. The story of an informant wasn't true, but Tuxhorn didn't know that. Now he could just stew over which one of his paid liars turned on him. It was turning out to be a really good day.

~~~

Stunned into silence, Charles walked out of the Sheriff's Office and into the unusually bright sunshine. For a minute, he couldn't even remember where he was. *This couldn't be happening...all my work...someone turned on him...losing everything...a new start...where?* He was beyond livid at the thought of a traitor among his so-called friends.

Sure, they were all low-life pigs. But they were paid well to lie in court. *How dare someone turn on Charles Tuxhorn?* Of course they would all deny it. They were pigs, not *stupid* pigs.

The sheriff was sure right about one thing. If he knew which one did it, he would kill him and take great pleasure in doing so.

Charles knew he wouldn't sleep that night. There was too many things to work out in his mind.

CHAPTER NINETEEN

The next few weeks were a haze for Eva. Charles would not tell her why they were going to move, only to get packed quickly.

"It's none of your business why we're going. Just pack. You don't like it? Then move in with your parents, but the kids and I are leaving." Charles was cruel and secretive as usual.

Eva finally found out from her family the reason for the move when she went to say goodbye to them. She took the three youngest children with her. The truth be known, she was afraid Charles would disappear with her children if she left them all alone.

It was so good to hug her parents again. She could only wonder if she would ever get another chance. She was delighted to find a couple of her siblings were also there to say goodbye.

William and Bartha were thrilled to see the little ones, as well as their mother. They filled her in on the latest scandal Charles had caused with the divorce.

"Honey," William said, "no one believed those lies about you. No one. Those buzzards were paid to say those things and now everyone knows it. Seems one of them talked and the sheriff gave Charles an ultimatum, jail or leave. If it had only been jail, we would all be free of him."

It was the first time in the county's history a wealthy farmer was told to get out or go to jail. Eva was stunned the sheriff didn't believe the lies told against her in court and that Charles was looked down upon for it. Someone had stood up for her! It didn't matter who, just that someone had. *Why couldn't it just have been jail?* The thought brought a grin to her sad face. How close she and the children had come to being free of him.

William told Eva about another bit of information the community had kept hidden from her now ex-husband. Charles' firstborn, John, now about twenty years old, was making a name for himself, and a good one at that.

Amanda and John had lived with her parents all his young life. His Uncle Gregory gave him the stability and father figure he needed. When John was twelve, his mother passed away, and he and his grandparents moved in with Gregory.

Amanda went to an early grave, apparently due to internal organs damaged at the hands of Charles Tuxhorn. Living only to protect her handsome son, she enrolled him in school under his grandmother's maiden name, Preston.

Eva was told Amanda knew Charles would kill her son, if he ever ran into him. John was never made aware of his father's true identity, living under the assumption that Mr. Preston had died close to the time he was born. Having acquired his mother's sweet personality, he grew up a happy boy who had a lot of friends, both in school and the community.

Once again, the entire community came to the aid of Amanda. When she enrolled John C. Preston in school at age five, the name was never questioned. When she called herself Mrs. Preston, it was never challenged. They all knew what had happened.

It was unseemly for a young lady to let herself be seduced like that, but the beating she took was all the punishment she should ever have to endure. One look at her damaged face, or the twist in her back, would tell any decent person that. They knew all right, but they weren't talking.

J.C., as John Charles was called, was working his way through school to be a veterinarian. Through the years of working with the local vet, Dr. Alonzo Merotti, a love of animals had enveloped his life. Dr. Al taught him well and knew he would make it through school just fine.

Gregory Buller was Amanda's brother, as well and a friend and pastor for the Whitworth's. He had told them the good doctor was helping with most of the school costs. The doc was supposed to be applying John's wages to the school fees, but Buller said Dr. Al always threw in much more to make sure there would be enough, should anything happen to him.

As his uncle, Gregory helped as he could. But as a preacher, he didn't make much and he had his own family to support as well as his parents, who were now elderly and frail. After Amanda died, his parents and J.C. had moved into the small rectory next to the church. It was crowded, but happy.

There wasn't a day went by that laughter wasn't heard pouring out their windows.

Gregory raised John as if he were his own. He loved the boy with all his heart. He couldn't help much financially, but he was always the father the boy needed. Since his wages went to his schooling, he would give the boy a little spending money from time to time so he could go to town with his friends.

J.C. grew up with loving and happy people. Tall and muscular, he was quick to laugh and saw the best in everyone. His parents gave him his good looks, but his personality came from his mother. His blue eyes were the first thing a person noticed, but his smile was a close second. Dr. Al said he was so good with animals because they would melt when he smiled at them. He swore to everyone it was true.

Eva had heard of J.C. Preston before, but never realized who he was. She was pleased to hear the news; genuinely happy to know John was raised with love and security. That's the way a child was supposed to be raised. It certainly would not have happened had Charles had his way all those years ago. When compared to the savage hatred her own children had been subjected to, she wanted to cry, but she felt a strange pride in her heart for J.C.

"Are you sure you want to leave with that animal?" Bartha Whitworth couldn't hold back the tears. Her momma was old now and not in good health. Eva knew she might not get much older.

"I can't leave the children, divorced or not. I would like nothing better than to leave Charles, Momma, but my children would not survive if I wasn't there." They all knew it was true, but hated to hear Eva say it.

They cried together, knowing the life she was trapped in, and now they didn't know if they would ever see her again. She also had something to say, before it was too late.

"I forgive you, Papa." Eva turned to face him. "I know you had my best interest at heart."

No one had to explain what she meant. She knew it was no secret about William paying Charles to marry her. He cried and held her close. No one could miss the scars on her face and hands from being beaten for the past twenty years.

"I don't know how you can, Eva," he was crying. "I know I can't forgive myself."

"There's nothing that can be done about it. I love you both. Write when you can."

Eva turned and left, knowing her lot in life was to protect her children until they could protect themselves. Then maybe she could come home and live in peace.

~~~

Charles was successful as a farmer. Whether the people liked him or not was not the issue. He knew as word of his leaving spread, they would line up to buy his first-rate equipment, fine stock, and finally, the farm itself. And he was right.

The house alone was better than most of his neighbors lived in. It wasn't the biggest or best in the county, but with the fine stone work, it was far better looking than most and he profited well from it. It was also well known his farm had produced fine crops.

When everything was sold, Charles made a trip to the bank in Nevada and changed all the money into gold coins. Bags and bags of gold coins. Charles had a passion for gold.

His hard work had paid off and Charles was a very wealthy man. Maybe moving somewhere else would be good after all. It would be a fresh start.

He figured no one would need to know about the divorce, so they would look respectable to everyone. Of course, Eva wasn't going to say anything, for it was a disgrace for a woman to be divorced by her husband, let alone for adultery. So they could pretend to be married, but Eva would still just be a servant of his. No one would know about his past difficulties with the law, either.

Where to go was an issue. Charles spent many nights lying awake pondering his new destination. Going south into Arkansas was an option, but he didn't like the idea of hot and humid working conditions. He loved the four seasons, but had no desire to return north to Illinois. There were too many bad memories.

So, what about Kansas?

His old man was dead, so he didn't have to deal with him. Maybe Charles should show up out there so his family could see how wealthy he had become. He had proven he didn't need any of them to succeed. The thought brought a smile to his face. Kansas it would be.

CHAPTER TWENTY

E va was showing with child. The wagon trip to Kansas in late 1900 was very difficult on her. A shadow of her young self, she had long ago given up, mentally and physically beaten down so far there was no climbing back.

She knew her children saw it and tried to help her. But Eva was supposed to be helping them survive their father, not them helping her. She had to stay strong for them. She just had to.

Her oldest child, Bertha, was now eighteen and took most of the responsibility for the young ones—Amos, only one year old, and Louis, nicknamed Budge, who was four. Her oldest son, Edward, was seventeen and helped when he could. Matilda was twelve, Mary was ten, and Blaine, eight. Then there was this eighth child on the way.

Reaching Inman, Kansas, was a relief for them all, but especially Eva. It was cold and slow going in the unusually early snowfall. Arriving at this time of year didn't exactly allow the countryside's beauty to stand out, either. The plains were barren and white, not at all like the rolling hills they were used to. But, she really didn't care about what was seen, only how ill she was feeling.

~~~

Charles couldn't wait to get everyone in a boarding house so he could get away from them all. He went straight to the county clerk's office and inquired as to the land other Tuxhorns owned and what was currently for sale.

Sight unseen, he chose to purchase eighty acres located several miles away from his mother's farm and that of his brother Leo Lewis Tuxhorn, whose property adjoined his mother's. The last thing he needed was having their noses constantly in his business. He paid with gold and filed the deed all in one afternoon.

Now it was time to see their new home. He loaded the wagon once again and they all left town.

The farm was actually magnificent but the house, while good sized, was old and weathered. Charles figured Eva and the kids didn't deserve any better so he paid particular attention to all of their conversations for any criticism of their new home. One complaint and he would force them to sleep outside. Then, they would see the house wasn't bad at all. Unfortunately, no one said a bad word, at least not that he heard.

Despite the age of the house, the four bedrooms were helpful. All the girls, Bertha, Matilda and Mary took one room, Edward and Blaine another. The youngest ones, Amos and Budge, were tucked into the smallest bedroom.

While the house might have been old, the barn was not. Charles was elated that it had recently been built, and was oversized to boot. It would hold more animals and equipment than the one he had in Missouri.

The next morning, Charles took Edward to purchase livestock and equipment. He also hired some help to work fencing for the winter and the land in the spring.

All the equipment and livestock settled in for the winter. The move to Kansas was complete.

~~~

His children were getting older and harder to control. They would all attack him with fists, pounding, trying to get him to stop punishing one kid. He would then turn on the next one closest to him. A fist or whatever was handy was the punishment of the moment. But the older ones were getting to be a problem.

How he would like to wipe them all off face of the earth. Some of his beatings left the child or children badly hurt, but that wasn't going to stop them from doing their chores on time. Those kids weren't living off him free and easy.

Charles remembered one time when Budge was playing outside the barn. He came out carrying a pipe and couldn't resist whacking the kid on the back of the head with it. He went down like a rock. He was five years old at the time, as he recalled. The kid lay unconscious for almost an hour and he never seemed quite right after that.

Budge wasn't brain dead or anything, he was just…well, goofy. That was the only way Charles could explain it to himself. The kid always had a silly grin on his face, expected everyone to like him, and just lived in his own happy little world.

Budge wasn't even afraid of him anymore. Nothing negative seemed to register with the kid. Charles was so taken back by the change that he didn't bother Budge after that. In fact, he hardly acknowledged he was there.

He never used a pipe on a kid's head again, either. He didn't want to have a bunch of idiots who couldn't do their chores, just sitting around, grinning.

Edward concerned him, though. He was much older now than Charles was when he challenged his father. He would not—could not— allow such a thing to happen to him. He would never let a kid get the best of him. Never. He had to figure out a way to make sure it didn't happen.

~~~

On a clear cold Monday morning in January, 1901, Eva was alone in the house with her oldest, Bertha. Most of the children were in school, Amos and Budge were taking a nap, and Charles was in town with Edward buying supplies.

"Momma," Bertha said in a low voice, "I want to leave, Momma. I can't stay here any longer. Each beating gets worse. I know you are going to have that baby in a couple of months.

I would like to be here to help you, but I just can't. I have never seen anyone hate another human being like Poppa hates me."

They both pulled out a chair and sat down at the table. Eva took a deep breath before speaking. She had been pregnant so many times she was not concerned about help with this baby. It would be nice, but not necessary.

"Honey, he hates everyone, as you well know. But you remind him of me, which is why he is extra hard on you." Eva loved her firstborn so much, but knew she needed to leave.

Almost choking on the words, she said, "Where would you go? What would you do?"

"I thought I would go back to Missouri to relatives. If that doesn't work out, I will go to Illinois where my uncles are. I am sure I can get work doing something, Momma. I know I can legally leave, I just want your blessing." Bertha started to cry.

Eva knew her daughter was barely holding it together. She also knew the girl had come all this way just so she could help her during this pregnancy. It was time Bertha looked after herself. It wouldn't be easy, but Eva would have to let her go.

She came around the table and put her arms around her child and kissed her on the top of her head. "Bertha, of course you have my blessing. I want what is best for you and staying here certainly isn't it."

Tearing herself away from the hug, she walked over to the kitchen sink with her back toward Bertha. With her arms braced on the sink, she hung her head in thought. After a couple of moments, she turned and said, "But I have one favor to ask of you. The last one I will ever ask."

Bertha stood up and looked Eva in the eyes and said, "Momma, anything. I will do anything you ask."

Eva walked toward her daughter. Looking into Bertha's eyes, she spoke.

"I want you to take Tilly with you."

Matilda was only twelve years old. The look on Bertha's face told Eva she was surprised and didn't understand the request.

"Tilly isn't strong like the rest of you are, Bertha. She is gentle in nature and can't handle the violence in this household. Remember last month when Poppa grabbed her off the floor by her arm? Her fear was so great; she just passed out while hanging there. What if next time, her little heart gives out?"

Tilly was fragile and soft spoken. She didn't seem to have the ability to handle any stress at all. Eva knew Bertha was thinking about the legality of what she had asked her to do. She wanted to put her mind as ease quickly.

"I will give you a note saying I give you permission to take your sister. It wouldn't do any good if anyone challenged it. You know I don't have custody of you kids, but not many know that. But I don't think anyone would give it a second thought. You'll be okay since you are eighteen. Will you do it?"

"Of course I will, Momma. I don't want Tilly hurt either. When should we go?"

Having had a couple of moments to think about it, Eva was thrilled to see Bertha seemed actually glad she wouldn't be alone.

As the oldest, Bertha had been like a mother to all the younger kids anyway. Maybe having her sweet little sister with her would be like having her own daughter. Eva almost choked at the thought of losing them both at the same time. But right now, there were more important things to consider.

Eva was quickly calculating the timing involved to give her girls time to escape.

"Charles is leaving Thursday morning to go to McPherson to arrange for more cattle. He won't be back until Friday night, maybe Saturday morning if he stays for a few drinks. That means laundry will have to be done Wednesday for him." Eva spoke out loud as she was thinking.

"Your laundry will be done at the same time. After Charles is gone, you could leave with Tilly. That would give you a two-day head start."

Eva assured Bertha that her decision was the right one and the rest of them would be just fine. She even said with fewer children around, she probably could get more work done. That seemed to brighten Bertha's mood.

Eva set about to gather eggs. She was putting together a plan to protect herself when all this happened. She just prayed it would work.

~~~

Two days later, on Wednesday, laundry was done as expected. That evening, Eva asked Charles if she could go into town the next morning and sell some eggs to buy flour. He normally didn't like her leaving the house when he wasn't home, so she was holding her breath waiting for his answer.

Surprisingly, he didn't hesitate. With his usual nasty nature, he told her she had better get flour, because if they ran out, it would be her fault.

"And you know how I deal with your stupid mistakes," Charles threatened, giving her the permission she needed.

On Thursday morning, January 17, 1901, Charles rode off. Bertha bundled up Tilly and they walked off the farm. Eva kept the tears at bay until they were out of sight, letting them fall when she knew they wouldn't see or hear.

Some tears fell for losing her daughters, some for losing the only household help she had, and some in happy relief that two of her own were finally safe. She took the buggy into town and sold her eggs for flour.

Charles actually came home Saturday night, without any explanation for his extra time away. However, it was Monday night before he even noticed Bertha wasn't there. When asked about it, Eva said she was gone Thursday when she got back from town with the flour.

Furious, Charles shouted, "Why didn't you tell me?"

Eva knew every word from now on had to be convincing in order to quell any violence. She had to sound upset at her daughter.

"Why should I? You don't care if she is here or not. I am the one that's mad at her. She was the only help I had around here! How dare she leave me like this? I have a baby on the way and she knew I needed her." Eva intentionally sounded indignant, angry, and it was easy to let the tears fall. All the while, she kept her back to her husband as she busied herself in the kitchen.

Staring at the back of her head, Charles was silent for a moment. Eva was sure he would come up behind her and hit her. She was just waiting for the pain. She wasn't aware of the fact she had stopped breathing.

"Well, good riddance. She was worthless anyway. And you stop your whining, you cow. You don't deserve any help. Get your work done or I will kick you outa here and get someone who will." With that said, Charles left the house, slamming the door, and headed for the barn. Bertha leaving would make it harder on Eva, and she knew he liked that idea.

When the door slammed, Eva took her first deep breath... and smiled. Nothing had even been said about Tilly.

~~~

Bertha and Tilly made it to Missouri. It wasn't easy walking in the bitter cold, but Bertha knew it would be worth whatever sacrifice was needed. Their relatives in Missouri were kind enough to buy them railroad tickets to go on to Springfield, Illinois, where they would be farther away from harm. Once there, Bertha's relatives did take them in.

In a short time, both sisters found jobs at the Concordia College and moved into dorm rooms. They flourished both physically and emotionally. Bertha knew the beatings, the violence, and the sheer terror of growing up with Charles Tuxhorn was over for them. She hoped, for Tilly's sake, that the escape came soon enough for the little girl to allow at least a measure of healing. As for herself, she knew the memories would follow her to her grave.

~~~

A month after Bertha and Tilly left, Edward, aged seventeen, disappeared from the Tuxhorn farm. One morning he went out to work the fields with his father and never came back. At seventeen, Edward was certainly old enough to leave without much of a fight. But to leave without telling anyone where he was going, didn't seem right. Edward wouldn't do that. Not only did he not say goodbye, but he didn't even take his clothes.

The battles between Edward and his father were well known. Edward fought back as best he could, but he always ended up waking up right where he had been coldcocked. The fact of the matter was a bad argument *had* been heard between the two of them by Frank Gamm the day Edward was last seen.

Frank didn't want to get into his neighbor's business any more than needed, so he never went over the small hill, that separated their property, to check it out. But they sure were screaming obscenities. What a way to live. Frank couldn't imagine it.

Charles told everyone Edward ran away. He even complained that Edward had gotten old enough to get some real work out of him and he just took off. Since this was on the heels of Bertha leaving, his story was never questioned.

CHAPTER TWENTY-ONE

Eva was glad her three oldest were now away from their father. At least, she thought Edward had gotten away. Now all she had to do was get her four youngest out of his reach. Safely away from Charles...what a wonderful thought. *Please, God, let me see that day.* Eva also had her unborn to think of and feared her husband more whenever she was with child. How easily his temper could end a precious life before it began.

She was wearing down this time. It was her eighth pregnancy, but she knew this one was different. It seemed this baby was testing her strength. After her chores were done, she would lie down in the small room she now shared with her youngest, Amos.

After the oldest three had left, Budge was put in a bedroom with Blain and Eva was in a bedroom with little Amos, and Mary took the smallest room. Charles slept in the big bedroom by himself. She didn't care; she liked being away from him and able to talk with her youngest child.

When things became really bad with his poppa, Amos would run into the room and crawl under the bed to hide until it was over. He was so little. He certainly knew what was going on, but he didn't know why.

Eva would try and comfort him with her voice, but she didn't dare cuddle him in her arms if Charles was around. If he caught them, he would beat Amos for sure. He hated his children feeling any kind of love. She didn't know why, but it didn't matter anymore after all this time.

She continued to lose weight even as her belly filled out with child. She never was a big woman, slender in build and only about five feet four inches tall. Growing up, she had been stronger than she looked, being able to carry her share of firewood as well as milking the cows. That seemed a world ago and another life. *What had happened to that innocent girl? So happy and carefree...*

Sure, there were times she was concerned she would never have a suitor, but she was happy just helping her momma and poppa. Playing with her little siblings was a joy. How she loved them all.

The baby was heavy. She knew her time was coming soon. This one hadn't been active like her others. Maybe she was going to have a quiet baby. Wouldn't that be nice? At least this child would be her last. Charles hadn't touched her since the divorce. Some clouds did come with silver linings. Normally she would be appalled at the thought of having a child out of wedlock, with no father. But it was so much more wonderful than the alternative. Just ask any of her kids...

~~~

March of 1901, Eva went into labor. Dr. Blake stopped by, but there wasn't much he could do. The boy, she named Henry, was stillborn leaving Eva weak and bedridden.

She was painfully absent at her infant son's funeral, two days later, but many showed up to show respect for a life that never had a chance.

Among those at the funeral, Charles spotted a pretty lady dabbing tears from her eyes. Afterward, she and her parents came over to express their condolences for his loss and to inquire as to Eva's health.

They were Mr. and Mrs. John Friesen and their children. Charles patiently acknowledged each introduction, from the youngest child to the oldest, until they finally came to their nineteen-year-old daughter, Aganetha.

"Then here's our pretty Aganetha. We call her Nettie for short." John Friesen moved on to his oldest son, but Charles was no longer listening. *Nettie.* He could hardly take his eyes off her.

She was about five feet eight inches tall and had padding on her bones. Not like Eva, who was short, skinny, and small boned. When she smiled at him, Charles was pretty sure he melted. He had never felt this way in his entire life. *Who was this Nettie?* All he could do was smile back.

At forty-five years old, Charles was still handsome and had all the looks a woman could want, plus the strong lean body only hard work on a farm could produce. Almost six feet himself, he could look her straight in the face, since she was tall. Wow, what an experience. Being twenty-six years her senior never crossed his mind. What difference did that make?

From that moment on, Nettie Friesen never left his mind. It was a new feeling, but Charles felt affection for another human being.

~~~

Leo Lewis and his wife, Ida, were present at the baby's funeral. Even though he was Charles' younger brother, they had only spoken a few times since he moved to Kansas. Leo just couldn't condone the violent nature he saw in his oldest brother.

Whatever the problem was, just being around Charles made Leo feel uncomfortable. The brothers never invited each other over for dinners or celebrations. That didn't mean he wouldn't mourn the loss of a child. It just wasn't right. Little Henry didn't have a chance at life. No, it just wasn't right.

It seemed the nature of a funeral was where old memories were stirred up, and this one was no different for Leo. He was only four years old when Charles left to go live elsewhere. Raised without Charles around, they didn't have a history to share. He really didn't remember much about his brother, except his pretty blue eyes. They were certainly still blue, but now he could swear there was evil in them. During his youth, his mother never mentioned Charles nor allowed anyone else to. Leo was beginning to see why.

His mother, Elizabeth, didn't come with him today. She didn't feel up to the crowd of people. Leo noticed Charles didn't bother asking about her. The Tuxhorns didn't have much interaction as a family. Which made it hard to believe, but once they actually got together for a family photo. *Family photo? Some family!* Leo shook his head.

It was funny how a photo of a bunch of people couldn't reveal the true feelings in their hearts. There was no love lost between Charles and his Mother and everyone knew it. He didn't know why, but it had been that way since as far back as he could remember.

Mother owned three times more land than Charles, with two hundred and forty acres. Leo owned another one hundred and sixty acres that attached to her farm. He worked all four hundred acres and they wanted for nothing. They were doing well.

Leo had to admit, Charles owned a nice farm, but the thing that really made the man wealthy was all the small farms he bought and then sold to folks on payments. He'd write up a contract, just like a bank, and the new owners would make their payments to him. Charles was getting money for land he didn't even have to work.

Charles was clever, that was for sure, but Leo was glad his brother lived several miles away. The farther away he was, the better, really.

It was still too bad about the baby, though. Their pastor had told them that baby Henry was already in Heaven with Jesus, and that was comforting to know.

~~~

Many neighbors came to show respect and mourn the loss of baby Henry. The Knackstedts, Postiers, and Weigands were just a few of those who took time out of their busy schedules.

Neighbors from all over the county brought food and offered to watch the children while Charles nursed his wife back to health. The food was accepted but the rest was firmly rejected. Those kids didn't need any pampering and he wasn't going to sit around and wait on Eva like he was her slave. That wasn't the way it was supposed to be.

~~~

In the two weeks after the baby's funeral, the doctor came back twice to check on Eva, but she wasn't rallying as he'd hoped she would.

"Charles," Dr. Blake said, "your wife may never be totally strong again. This baby really took it out of her."

Charles did his part to look concerned. "I know you have done everything you can, Doc. I really appreciate it. She means so much to all of us."

"I know," the doc said. "Keep a cool rag on her forehead and make sure she gets enough to eat so she can build up her strength again. Be patient."

With a nod, Charles showed him to the door and watched him ride off in his wagon. He was completely disgusted. Who was going to cook and clean? Who was going to wash the clothes? This useless wench was not going to just lie around and be waited on!

At the age of eleven, Mary was the oldest at home, so Charles told her she had the job of dealing with all the cooking, cleaning, and taking care of her younger siblings. Until her mother was back on her feet, he made it clear that it all fell on her.

Some evenings, Charles would go into Eva's room and they would hear him yelling. He demanded she get up and make herself useful. Eva's voice could not be heard, but they all heard their father. He yelled that she might as well be dead if she was going to be useless.

A few days after the doctor's last visit, Charles learned something that twisted his gut. Dropping by the feedlot in town, one afternoon, he heard two men talking.

"Jason, I'm telling you not to play house with that floozy. She'll get you dead to rights." Harry Belton was a merchant from McPherson.

"Harry, she's just gonna cook and wash my socks. I don't see the harm. It's not like I'm gonna marry her or anything." Jason was leaning his back against the fence.

"It's the Common Law Marriage thing, Jason. You could find yourself married to her before long," Harry said.

"'Cuse me, boys. I don't mean to interrupt, but I heard you mention something that interested me. What is this common marriage thing?" Charles could be charming when he wanted something and he was now all ears.

"It's called Common Law Marriage. In the state of Kansas, if you call yourself man and wife, then you are!" Harry repeated. Then he went on, "You living with a gal?"

"No, not me. I was just thinking of a cousin who just moved a squaw in with him. They didn't go to a judge or a preacher, so how could they be married?" Charles couldn't let them know why he was concerned.

"Does he call her his wife and does she agree with that?"

"Yeah, I guess so," Charles answered.

"Then in the eyes of the state of Kansas, they are married. They could be together only a couple of days and that don't matter. They're legally married." Both Harry and Jason swung up onto their horses. They said their goodbyes to Charles and rode off.

Charles' mind buzzed with this new information. *Could it really be true? What had he gotten himself into?* His mind went back over the time and expense of getting his divorce. Not to mention being kicked out of the entire state for doing so! *Had he gone through all of that crap in Missouri for nothing?*

Really? Kansas recognized Charles and Eva as legally married? Is this some kind of joke? He got a divorce in Missouri and Kansas law say they are married again. This can't be happening to me. It can't be!

What tortured Charles the most was whether Eva knew about this law. If she did, how she must have laughed behind his back. Was she going to make trouble for him again? Did she know she could take his farm?

For over twenty years, this woman had been a horrible yoke around his neck. He could actually feel the dark veil of rage wrap around him like a fog and not let go. It was time to eliminate the problem.

Approximately three weeks after baby Henry died, Charles told Amos to go sleep with his brother Budge for the night. This had never happened before and all the children took notice. He said their mother needed some time alone if she was going to get any better.

Amos was startled, but Charles knew happy-go-lucky Budge would think it was a great idea—but then, he would have thought the same about eating cow pies.

There was not any arguing from their mother's room that night. All was quiet. The following morning, while walking out the front door, Charles calmly announced to all the children, "Your mother's dead. Stay out of her room." He left, shutting the door behind him.

~~~

Dead? Momma's dead? She was sitting up yesterday afternoon. Mary remembered she even ate a small bowl of soup, which was more than she had been able to in the past week. Now she was dead. They all cried as they did their chores. The only love they had known was gone.

~~~

Dr. Blake was surprised when Tuxhorn rode into town to let him know his wife had died.

"Don't know what happened, Doc. She seemed to be doing fine, and then...." Tuxhorn told him. Doc could see he could hardly speak of this tragedy.

"Charles, only God knows about these things. My heart goes out to you and them young ones, but you will have to get on without her." Doc was doing his best to bring some comfort. These were never easy times for him. Trying to bring some comfort to the family after losing a loved one never seemed to get any easier. "Don't worry about the coroner. I'll get him out there for you."

As Dr. Blake walked toward the coroner's office, he saw Maltby watching him from his office window. Doc knew he would be wondering who had passed on this time.

"Hey, you need to get out to the Tuxhorn farm and pick up the Missus." Blake knew he had to make it as plain as possible.

"Tuxhorn? It was that nice lady? That's too bad, Doc." Coroner Maltby looked saddened.

"I didn't tell Charles, of course, but I knew there was a chance his wife might die." The doctor began musing in his own medical world. "Apoplexy is always a possibility...had to be what it was...thought she was better, but.... Just stopped breathing. Hmmm, too bad."

Suddenly, the doc realized he was thinking out loud.

"Sorry, Maltby." Blake spoke with certainty this time. "Go ahead and write it up. It was apoplexy.

"I told Tuxhorn you would pick her up today. He wants the funeral tomorrow. I know that seems awfully quick, but I expect he is not wanting to drag out the grief for him and his kids, especially right on the heels of that baby being born dead." Dr. Blake was saddened by it all.

"No problem, Doc." Maltby said. "Tomorrow is a bit quick, but since you say it was apoplexy, I don't need to spend a bunch of time trying to figure it out. There shouldn't be any reason the funeral can't be tomorrow."

Dr. Blake was one of the few who attended the funeral the next day. He watched as Evalee Tuxhorn, only thirty-nine years old, was buried next to her infant son. He was shocked to learn her children were not allowed to attend.

CHAPTER TWENTY-TWO

Fewer people were at Eva's funeral than had attended her son's. Most people didn't even know of her passing, until it was too late. There was no fanfare and it was apparent to all that Charles wanted it over quickly.

Frank Gamm wanted to be there to pay his final respects to a woman he knew was a kindly soul. The problem was Frank knew he would arouse the wrath of that devil Tuxhorn in order to do it. He was the man Charles hated with all of his might.

Being the immediate neighbor to the north of Charles, when he beat his kids, they sometimes ran to Gamm's farm to hide. He and his wife would feed them and dress their wounds before sending them back home.

Frank didn't normally get into another man's personal affairs, but he knew Charles was taking the punishment of his children way too far. Some of the wounds he had seen on those kids could have been life threatening, if not cared for. He was glad they came to him for help. Someone had to be there for them, and it sure wasn't their father.

Whenever he was in town, Frank would stop by the Sheriff's Office and let them know the last time the young ones came running to him for medical attention and temporary safety. He didn't like putting a name tag on anyone, but he felt Charles was one sick pig.

The sheriff always told him none of it was news, but Frank would tell them anyway. It seemed his description of Tuxhorn was a whole lot nicer than what some other folks had to say. Almost everyone knew about his violent temper, and the terms "insane" and "psychopath" came up a lot.

Frank was a quiet, God-fearing man, and he knew half beating children to death was not what God meant when He said, "spare the rod, spoil the child." He raised his family in the church and tried to live a good Christian life, but that Tuxhorn did try his patience. He even doubted his neighbor would ever see a grandchild, since he had no qualms stomach punching the girls the same as the boys. It almost made him ill to think of all the things those kids went through.

Watching the few people gathered around Eva's grave, he remembered how his frustrations at Tuxhorn had gotten the better of him one night. Frank went for a walk alone out past his barn to keep from letting his family see his dismay.

The night was beautiful, clear, and the stars were sparkling. Such evenings always put him in awe of such a glorious God. He stood looking at the sky for a moment and then said aloud, "Lord, why did you put Tuxhorn on that farm south of me? Don't I have troubles enough? I know there is evil in this world, but I sure didn't expect it to live next door."

The stars twinkled back at him until peace returned to his troubled heart. Then he knew God had answered his questions. He just knew. If it weren't for him helping out, a couple of those kids would probably be dead by now. Frank smiled, thanked God for His Grace, and went back into his house a much happier man.

He would never turn one of the Tuxhorn children away, now or ever. He just wouldn't do it.

When Charles found out about each time Frank and his wife helped the children, he would throw a tantrum. He would race his horse over to Frank's house, barely able to pull to a stop at his porch. Then Charles would just sit there berating and threating him. That violent temper and despicable foul language seemed to be all the man knew, and Frank couldn't get a word in edgewise.

"You stay away from my kids, you slimy pig. If you touch them again, I will kill you! You hear me? Those kids are mine and you have no right to interfere." Charles didn't even get off his horse. Gamm would see him coming and come out onto the front porch.

"Charles, I don't want any trouble. But you can't beat those…."

"I can do whatever I *please!* Keep your nose out of my business!" Charles would ride away; seemingly hating Gamm more each time, if that was even possible.

"What do you think you are doing here?"

The venom in the voice startled Frank back into the present. Turning around, he saw Charles had finally noticed he and his wife were here at Eva's funeral. Charles was walking over to him as fast as he could with his hand on his holstered gun. Frank's wife stepped behind him in fear.

"I want no trouble, Tuxhorn. We just wanted to pay our respects to your wife. We didn't know her well, but heard she was a fine lady." Frank tried to explain, but he could see it wasn't going to work. Maybe coming to her funeral was not such a good idea after all.

"Get out of here or I will put a bullet in your head." Charles spoke through gritted teeth, low, so no one else could hear.

"We're leaving," Frank said, shaking his head in total frustration. He tipped his hat at a couple of other people he knew at the funeral who were farther away, but watching the confrontation, then he turned back at Charles. He looked him right in the eye and, through his own gritted teeth, said, "Sorry for your loss." The Gamm's walked away, got into their buggy, and went home.

Frank could see Charles was seething. He also knew without a doubt, as sure as the sun would come up tomorrow, Charles would try to kill him one day. He silently said a prayer for God to help him when that terrible day comes.

~~~

As the children struggled to get along without their mother, Mary noticed her father was spending more and more time away from the house. Left to fend for themselves, she tried to comfort the three younger ones when they became frightened. She would sing happy songs to build up their spirits when the loss of their mother brought tears. Somehow, they had to make it. Mary was glad their father wasn't spending much time in the house, but it only made it clearer they were alone in the world.

~~~

Charles spent every waking moment trying to figure out how to see Nettie Friesen again. She had become an obsession that stole his thoughts. His feelings for her were out of control. He was astounded by what love really felt like. Did anyone else in the entire world feel as he did? He sincerely doubted anyone would understand.

One thing standing between him and Nettie was her family. John H. Friesen and his family were devout Mennonites, a religious group not quite as strict as the Amish, but strict enough. Because of his obsession with Nettie, he had to learn as much about them as he could.

The Mennonites were a peaceful people and tended to be more tolerant of technology and the outside world than the Amish. They accepted higher education and modern technology because they saw these influences as ways to strengthen their religious beliefs.

The Amish, on the other hand, tended to feel those influences of the outside world only interfered with the purity of their faith. They generally forbade higher education, and dressed in "plain" clothes.

Both were born out of the Anabaptist sect from Germany and Holland. Anabaptists were against baptizing a baby at birth, as was the case in the Catholic religion.

Amish and Mennonites felt a person had to make that choice for himself when he was old enough to understand what he was doing. Going against the church of the day was no small thing and many died in Europe for their beliefs. Religious freedom was the main reason most people emigrated to America.

Not that any of this mattered to Charles. Religion was for the ignorant who needed a fairy tale to believe in. He wasn't going to die for believing in something that stupid. The whole Mennonite thing was a major irritation.

How could any idiot think there was a God sitting on a cloud somewhere watching everything? Where was this wonderful watchdog when *he* was born? And that Bible book—people read it over and over. Why? Any book he had ever read, he only needed to read it once. It showed how dumb those people were.

Charles couldn't believe some of the moronic things people fell for. It didn't make sense to him and never would. Those fools used the excuse that it was Sunday to keep from working. Well, he was not going to be a dirt-eating pauper. He wouldn't work on Sunday when he saw God come down and do the work for him. But, now he had gone and fallen for a Mennonite girl. It was some kind of cruel joke.

Much to his relief, however, Charles noticed Nettie did not seem to fit the mold of a proper Mennonite young lady. She didn't act like the conservative people he had so quickly learned about. She flirted openly with him, to the chagrin of any family member close by. He had no doubt she knew all about his reputation.

When he saw her in town or riding toward home, he would try to get close enough to speak to her. When she spotted him—after making sure no kin was watching—she would run over to talk with him. Charles knew she liked his company and it was enough to make a man go off the deep end.

Once, she even leaned over and pecked him on the cheek before running off at the sound of her father calling. His heart raced for two hours afterward. No, this was no Mennonite girl. This was *his* girl.

During the summer after Eva died, Charles brought in a healthy crop, so good. in fact. it made the local newspapers:

"Chas. Tuxhorn threshed last week. He had over 1500 bushels on 55 acres. Borneman and Walters report it was the best quality they have threshed." August 23, 1901, Inman, Kansas.

He was a good farmer, no one could deny that. Charles hoped such praised was not lost on Nettie.

His large barn had a room separated in back where he could go to drink, sleep, or just get away from Eva and her brats. He kept it locked and told the hired hands they were not to touch it. There was a lot of speculation among the employees, but no one was brave enough to get close to that door.

Charles had furnished it with a high-quality bed and chair. It was nicer than anything in the house, because it was for him. Eva hadn't deserved anything this nice. The small window was high, for privacy, but let in nice afternoon light. There was a cabinet with some liquor in it, a porcelain washbasin on top and an extra shotgun or two against the walls. A large oil lamp on the small table next to the bed made the night simply disappear when he wanted it to. It was comfortable and private, as well as his favorite place to be.

Charles also had a one-room shack on the back of his property, but it wasn't much. The original settlers had probably built it as their house way back in the old days. It was small and not useable for more than a storage area.

He already had to replace the one small broken window and even put iron railings over the outside so the birds flying into it wouldn't break it again. But it was good for storing tools when working in the fields. That way, he didn't have to ride all the way back to the barn to get them.

He still needed to work on the floor of the shack, but it would all be done in due time. Since it was so far away from the main house, he put a heavy barn latch and lock on the outside of the only door, so thieves wouldn't break in, though that never worried him much. Steal from him and everyone knew it would be a fast track to being dead, and he liked it that way. Fear was the perfect motivator to Charles.

But he never wanted Nettie to fear him. What he wanted from her was different.

Nettie deserved the best he could give her and, with his money, that was a lot. All she had to do was ask and he would get it. Maybe she would want one of those noisy automobiles people were showing up with. He thought they were stupid things, but if that was what she wanted, he would buy her one. She stayed on his mind all the time.

One afternoon, he walked into the feed store and nearly knocked her down as she was coming out. As soon as she saw him, she put on a big smile and slowed her exit. When he left the store, she was only a few feet down the path looking into another store window. He walked up behind her. They watched each other in the window reflection. He smiled and she smiled. How he wanted to touch her. This woman was driving him crazy.

Leaning forward to whisper into her ear, he said, "I have a lot of work to do in my barn this evening. I'll probably be there at least until ten."

Straightening up, he turned to walk away and said, "If anyone is interested."

It was a bold move, but he would do anything to be alone with her. Nettie was his whether she knew it or not. He would never let her go.

CHAPTER TWENTY-THREE

Charles told his farmhands to go home around eight that evening, even though it was still daylight, and they were glad to oblige. He had both ends of the barn open to give the pleasant evening breeze the opportunity to blow through like a comfortable sigh.

Putting a clean blanket over a bale of hay, he made a nice comfortable place for Nettie to sit and talk—that is, if she came. What if she didn't? His heart skipped as he thought of the possibility. Contemplating that dilemma, his thoughts were interrupted.

"I understand that a hard-working man lives here." Nettie's soft voice was music to his very soul.

Charles slowly turned around to see the woman who dominated his heart and world. "Well, I don't know about that, ma'am." He was smiling now. "But I reckon your presence would stop any work from getting done." Was he actually feeling a little shy?

"And why would that be, Mr. Tuxhorn?" Walking slowly toward him, Nettie's voice was teasing, sexy, and inviting.

"Well now, when someone as pretty as you shows up, no man in his right mind would be able to concentrate on his work." Charles was happier than he could ever remember. "Just what brings a nice woman like you into a dirty old barn?"

"Well, I heard a handsome widower was here who might like some company," Nettie said.

"Well, now… He surely would…he surely would." Charles closed the gap between them. Slipping his arms around her waist, he pulled her close. When their lips barely touched, he hesitated for a few seconds, teasing her with his lips, then kissed her as he had never kissed a woman before.

Nettie returned his passion just as eagerly. It was obvious they weren't going to spend any time chatting, so the blanket on the hay would not be needed. He grabbed her hand and opened the door to his private room. He pulled her in and down onto the comfortable bed. She didn't try to stop him. She seemed to want him as much as he wanted her.

The next hour was one of unleashed passion. Hardly any words were spoken. Charles was pleased she was a virgin, but if she hadn't been, he probably wouldn't have cared. He sure didn't know a woman could enjoy sex as much as a man did. They couldn't get enough of each other, but time was their enemy. Just when it seemed his life was beginning, it ended.

"I have to go. Pop will be looking for me," Nettie said as she got up and started dressing.

"Forget him," Charles said as he reached for her hand. "Stay here with me. Forever. I want you to be here. Pack up your things and move into the house." Charles had never meant anything so much in his life.

"With all of your children? I don't think that is a good idea." Nettie let out a little laugh with her sarcasm.

"Forget them! I don't care about any of them. I want *you*." The thought that he could lose Nettie over those brats of Eva's made his anger flare. It added to the hate he already felt for them.

Though not concerned, the violent change in his personality was not lost on her. Nettie smiled and said, "I'll think about it, Charles. Right now, I have to go."

"When can I see you again?" Charles didn't think he could wait very long.

"Soon." Nettie kissed him passionately on the lips, slipped out the door, and disappeared through the backside of the barn. Charles lay back on the bed for the next couple of hours going over every minute with her. No doubt about it, he was in love.

Nettie kept Charles updated as best she could on when she would be in town again or able to come by the barn for a while.

Once, when Nettie was shopping in the ladies' wear section of the mercantile store, Charles followed her around, thinking they would not be noticed. She looked at dresses and he commented on what he thought would look good on her. Of course, his choices were the ones that showed off her hourglass figure, and a lot of it, at that. But Nettie told him her family wouldn't allow her to buy something like that, let alone ever wear it.

The next time she went to visit Charles in his barn, she was shocked to find two new dresses hanging on newly installed hooks in their secret bedroom. Of course, they were ones Charles had wanted for her.

"Charles, they are beautiful. I love them! They are just the ones I would have chosen for myself," Nettie said.

"I hate dressing like a frump just because that's the way my family wants me to look. Why won't they just let me live my own life?" Nettie stuck out her lower lip in a pout. Charles thought it made her look cute.

She tried them on one at a time. After Charles fully admired each one, he would slowly strip it off. Nettie enjoyed standing naked in front of him. It was something he had never seen before. Women didn't completely undress in front of a man because it was unseemly, but Nettie did and it excited him more, if that was possible.

He spent hours just running his hands over her bare body like she was a fragile, porcelain doll. When it came down to sex, however, she proved she was not about to break. No matter what he wanted to do, she was a willing participant.

~~~

Throughout the fall of 1901, Charles and Nettie were seen openly with each other, no longer caring about the consequences. John Friesen was livid over the apparent nonchalance of his daughter and her quickly disappearing reputation. Bringing it up only made her laugh. What others thought of her didn't seem to matter one bit.

"What Charles thinks of me is all that matters, Pop. That's just the way it is."

But John could not allow this to continue; after all, he was the head of his household.

In December, Friesen drove his buggy over to the Tuxhorn farm to confront Charles about his wayward child. He found his nemesis at the front road, about to ride out for the day.

Friesen stepped down from his buggy and watched as Charles dismounted his horse and walked over. It was time John set things straight.

"Now see here, Tuxhorn. You can't continue to see my daughter. It ain't right. Her mother and I want her to settle down with a nice Mennonite boy her own age and…"

John Friesen didn't get another word out of his mouth. He saw the murder in Charles' eyes, but he also saw it too late.

~~~

Charles was leaving for the day to see about obtaining more cattle. He was surprised to see John Friesen at the road. He was getting out of his buggy, so Charles thought it would be better to get off his horse and see what the man wanted. He wasn't too crazy about this religious zealot who didn't like Nettie doing what she wanted, but he would find out the reason for this visit.

The man opened his mouth and stated he didn't want Charles to see Nettie any more. Rage exploded all over him.

The thought that this snake wanted to take Nettie away from him was beyond his ability to handle. This pig wanted her to have *sex* with a man her *own* age. He wanted another man to look upon her body as he had? Charles' intense hatred took control of his mind.

He started beating the man to a pulp. When he was down he kicked him and punched him some more. The only thing registering in his mind was murder. He had to kill the scumbag in from of him. Kill the pig who wanted to take Nettie away from him!

After the blood flowed and the vile man on the ground was apparently dead, Charles got back onto his horse and rode away, completely stunned that anyone would try to take Nettie away from him. *It was absolutely incredible.*

~~~

John Friesen would never remember everything that happened after the first few punches. During his beating, he went in and out of consciousness. John felt the continuing punches into his face, as well as the kicks aimed for his kidneys and groin. The pain was excruciating. At one point, in his delusion, he thought it was a demon that attacked him. Then he would see Charles' face again. Quietly, he cried to the Lord that if it was his time to please take care of his family. Finally, John's mind let go.

How long he lay by the road, no one knew for sure. Frank Gamm was riding home when he saw John's rig standing in the middle of the road. It was then Frank saw his body lying in the ditch. He picked John up as carefully as he could and put him in the back of John's own buggy. After Frank tied his horse on the back of the rig, he turned it around and headed back for town as fast as he dared.

John was barely alive, but thanks to Gamm, he was in the hospital in a coma, and the rig was back on the Friesen farm by nightfall. No one knew whether John would live or die.

Found lying in front of the Tuxhorn farm, there was little doubt about who had done this, but there would be no way of proving it. Charles could prove he was gone all day and John had not told anyone he was going to have a talk with Charles about leaving his daughter alone.

To announce that would have been humiliating for a Mennonite father whose girl was openly having sex with the devil. He hoped no more people would need to know if Charles would just stop seeing her.

~~~

John did survive the attack, but it took two weeks in the hospital and months at home to recover. Doc knew, however, that he would walk with a limp for the rest of his life.

"You can count your lucky stars this happened in December." Dr. Blake was walking John out of the hospital so he could go home to rest. "The cold air helped keep you alive. Had it been in the July heat, you most likely would have died after just a short time on that road." He helped John into a buggy and watched as he left for home with his wife.

Doc knew it was amazing the man had lived. He surely had a guardian angel watching over him. Could Tuxhorn have really done this? Could one human being really have done this much damage?

Suddenly, the doctor's thoughts raced back to Eva. Charles couldn't have had anything to do with that. Surely not. The unthinkable filled his heart with dread. Of course he couldn't have. He had heard a lot of the gossip about the man, but there wasn't any reason to think such terrible things about someone. The doctor shook the idea from his head and went back inside to work.

John Friesen told the sheriff Charles Tuxhorn had been the one who beat him. However, it was his word against that of Charles. Again, the sheriff was beside himself. No one could be charged. Just another crime that filthy dog would get away with.

~~~

The fact that Friesen lived was an irritation to Charles, but not a concern. He could prove he was somewhere else. And the beautiful part of it was while her father was in the hospital; Nettie packed up her things and moved into his house.

Granted, it was an immediate nightmare with those brats, but if he had to kill each one of them, they would learn to respect her.

Mary, now twelve, was in charge of the smaller children—Blaine nine, Budge was five and little Amos, who was only two.

He constantly had to warn them about not saying or doing anything to upset Nettie, but they wouldn't listen.

From the first moment there was constant fighting. Charles was vicious with the children. He demanded they wait on her every need. If Nettie was to tell him they didn't, the beatings would be fuelled by rage.

Charles was concerned that Nettie wouldn't like how he treated the kids, but he was thrilled to see she didn't seem to care what happened to them. It really wasn't her problem. She was truly a woman after his own heart.

When the kids caused her or Charles any problems, their rewards were bloody lips and black eyes. However, Charles knew Nettie was miserable. This worried him, because there was no way he was going to let those brats drive Nettie away from him.

~~~

In early 1902, Charles came up with the answer to his and Nettie's problem. On the opposite side of the farm, as far away from the old house he could get, he started building a nice new house for Nettie.

She was thrilled and spent most of her time in town ordering expensive new furniture. Openly living in sin with the man who attempted to murder her father, she was shunned by her family. However, she was not affected by it at all. She was right where she wanted to be.

The shopkeepers may not have liked her, but none of them refused to take the large amount of money Nettie spent.

When she thought of the Mennonite ways her parents wanted her to follow, it made her shudder. She had pretty things now. No one was going to take them away from her. She knew Charles was glad to give her anything she wanted.

The new house was finally ready in August. Nettie couldn't wait to move in. *Finally alone without all those brats of his.* What horrible kids they were. Now she would have Charles all to herself. He left the children in the old house to fend for themselves.

After Charles brought it up several times, she finally agreed to marry him, on one condition, of course. He had to swear she would not have to raise that "other woman's kids." Charles assured her that would never happen, so she said yes.

On September 23, 1902, after living in their new home for about a month, Charles and Nettie rode into McPherson, the county seat, and got married. She knew they were the happiest couple on earth.

~~~

It was a relief for the children when Poppa and Nettie moved out. They couldn't believe he married her, but that was another disappointment in their young lives. He would stop by the old house to give orders about the farm chores the kids had to do. He expected his demands to be followed to the letter, or someone would pay. They knew not to cross him.

The oldest two were forced to work the farm. When he got old enough, Amos would also be assigned chores. Budge did whatever Mary could figure out he was capable of. The children had no thought of refusing. Pain was the only option to disobeying Poppa's orders. They knew nothing else.

During the fall and winter of 1902, Charles would drop some groceries at the old house from time to time, but never on a regular schedule. The children never knew when food would appear, so they ate sparingly to save what they could. They didn't dare complain for fear the meager supplies would disappear altogether. Or even worse, there could be physical retaliation for complaining.

Throughout the fall, Mary and Blaine would scour the nearby farms for anything they could steal to eat. They would sneak over and load up their pockets, buckets, and arms—anything that could carry items home.

If any neighbors knew of the Tuxhorn children in their orchards or cornfields, they didn't say anything. The children only took what they could eat in the next day or two. Autumn found them healthy. When winter came, they lost weight.

CHAPTER TWENTY-FOUR

Charles and Nettie Tuxhorn were very happy together. He was totally affectionate and caring around his wife. He would do anything for her and she felt the same. For entertainment, they would have a pig roast over the huge fire pit set up behind the new house. They would invite all of the hands and their wives, if they had one, to come and share.

Most of the hired help on the Tuxhorn farm were ex-cons or lowlifes, but they were the only people who would agree to work for such a volatile boss. Charles didn't have a problem with paying a good wage for loyalty, so they all vied for the next project. The money wasn't the only thing to consider; there was also the fact that no one else would hire them with their backgrounds.

If one of their own didn't show up for work, they assumed the missing party wanted to move on. Their lifestyles were that of transients. A man might stay a month or a year. No one ever knew.

Joey Stark, a young man about twenty-eight-years-old, showed up wanting work. He only stayed about six months, but, during that time, he worked hard. One evening during a barbeque behind the house, Joey walked up to Nettie and said, "You look right purdy tonight, ma'am." He then went for another helping of pork.

Charles said he quit the very next day and left for places unknown. He said it was too bad, because he was a good worker. No one could figure out why he didn't take his horse or saddlebags. Everything he owned was still there. A person never knew what wandering folks will do.

The happy life with Nettie was offset for Charles by his constant temper with others. Hardly a month went by when he didn't turn on someone verbally or try to kill them with his bare hands.

What he did to John Friesen would not be forgotten in the county. Afterward, if a man absolutely needed to approach Charles for any reason, he would never do it alone. The reasoning was if an out-of-control Tuxhorn attacked, the second and third party was not only a witness, but could get the victim out of harm's way before it was too late. More often than not, people walked across the street to avoid him whenever they saw him coming.

The year 1903 rolled around and in the spring, Nettie discovered she was pregnant, due sometime in December. Charles was thrilled. He said he had the perfect life now and his young wife was going to have his child.

The children in the old house were not thrilled about the news, especially Mary. Was there going to be another baby for poppa to beat up? Was she going to have to raise that one, too? At almost thirteen, she just didn't think she could handle any more.

"If they think I am going to raise that kid of theirs, they can think again." Mary was near tears. Life just couldn't get any worse. No one loved her or her siblings, not since Momma died.

"I just won't stay here. I just won't." Mary had thought of it many times. What if she went to live with her older sister Bertha, or any other relative, for that matter? Surely it couldn't be any worse than this.

"Don't go frettin' about things you don't know about, Mary." It was Blaine, the sensible one. "Don't bring on the misery until you have to."

"Like you have to do the cooking and everything…I wish I was a boy." Mary was sick and tired, but mostly just tired.

They all went to school when they could, but some days they were forced to work the farm all day. They would read to each other at night and help teach Amos to read and write. He was still awfully young, but he was smart and catching on. He was too young for school but he had to go with Mary anyway, because she couldn't leave him home alone.

Blaine was the brains among them. He was very good at reading and writing. He just seemed to get it. He also had a way of avoiding a lot of Poppa's wrath. At least more than the rest of them could.

When it came to reading, Mary struggled with the big words, but she hadn't given up yet. Budge, at seven was also trying to learn. In his happy-go-lucky world, reading was not necessary. Mary was not too concerned with his lack of progress. She knew he may never really want to read.

It was little Amos that brought laughter to a sad house. Just three years old, Mary and Blaine felt like his parents, which in a literal sense, they were. When he fell, or learned a new word, they were there to help or praise. When he was hungry, they made sure he was fed first and then, if there was anything left, they would eat.

The whole thing saddened Mary. The only love Amos knew was from his siblings, but at least he had that. She was going to make sure he had that. At such a young age, Mary was feeling and acting like a mother.

Nevertheless, her mind kept coming back to this new baby. Surely they wouldn't force her to take on another one? On the other hand, maybe they wouldn't make her raise Nettie's baby. Maybe they would just go away and never come back.

~~~

Charles and Nettie were looking forward to their first child. A room was being prepared as a nursery. A boy baby would be named Clarence F. Tuxhorn. The F didn't stand for anything, but Nettie thought it sounded important. Otherwise, a girl would be Sarah Aganetha Tuxhorn.

Charles loved the cooler evenings on the porch of his new house. Nettie was cleaning up after supper and he took in the breeze. Life was mostly good. He had Nettie and that was all that mattered. People frowned upon them because she was the same age as his oldest kid, Bertha, now twenty. No matter. What others thought didn't concern him.

She made him feel young again, that was a fact. He'd had a lot of women in his day, but nothing the likes of Nettie in the bedroom. It seemed she couldn't get enough of him. *She could really tire a man out after a long day's work, but she was surely worth it.* The thought brought a smile on his face.

She had a nutty sense of humor and made him laugh. They were like two teenage kids together, pulling pranks whenever they could.

Earlier this evening, he came home to find her in the kitchen getting ready to fry up chicken. That would give him just enough time to clean up a bit before it hit the table. He snuck up behind her and grabbed her around the waist. She screamed and jumped right out of his arms.

"Charles Tuxhorn, you about scared me to death." She was always glad to see him.

"Well, who did you think it was?" Charles pulled her to him and was talking low. He brushed her lips with his. "So interested in that chicken that your old man can't touch his wife?"

Lips still close, she said, "I don't care about that stupid chicken. We can do other things before it gets fried." Her body was rubbing his, leaving no doubt about what she had in mind.

"Oh, no you don't!" Charles pushed her away, laughing. "You gotta feed me or I won't have the strength for you later." Now they both were laughing. Nettie went back to the stove and her chicken.

Yes, life was good with his young wife. They were going to have some good-looking children, no doubt about it. Not like those brats he had to put up with in the old house. They reminded him of the miserable years he was forced to spend with their mother. In his eyes, they were all ugly, just like her. He hated them. They were a constant reminder of his unhappy past and he didn't want the memories, or them, around.

Best thing he ever did was build this new house for him and Nettie. He could go days without having to think of the old house. They were no more than pitiful squatters. Living rent free on his land and always whining about wanting food or clothes for school. Didn't they know they had to earn their own way like he did?

He would run them all off, but there was no way he was going to send them to some relative's lap of luxury where they would be coddled into useless pigs. Besides, they didn't deserve to be happy any more than their mother did.

They wanted to live in that old house—they were going to have to work his farm to pay for it. Anger welled up in him every time he thought of Bertha being gone when she was old enough to put in more hours a day.

She went off to relatives and told all those lies about him. Rumors about him came drifting back from Illinois. Charles wanted to slap her face for even mentioning his name. What gave her the right?

He wasn't cruel to those stupid kids. They were the ones who were no good. He gave them what they deserved. Charles knew the only thing he could do was keep an eye on those at home. Making them work before and after school would keep them busy and out of his hair.

Charles could hear Nettie finishing up in the kitchen, and knew she would pour them each a drink and join him on the porch in a few minutes. She was humming a tune he didn't know.

Something he had been thinking about came back to mind. Mary had turned thirteen, so he would make her quit school and stay on the farm to work. Charles smiled at the thought. She wouldn't like it, but he didn't care. What a pain she was, always whining about not enough food, or she couldn't work the farm and tend her siblings, too. What a lazy piece of trash she turned out to be, like her mother. Of course, none of the others seemed to be any better.

If he tried to make the younger ones stay home, the law would get involved. It was hard to believe but the state of Kansas had a despicable law that kids had to go to school until they were thirteen. When did it happen that the government could say what a man could or couldn't do with his own kids? That was not supposed to happen in America. It was another law in Kansas he didn't like.

Just thinking about it made his blood boil. He owned those kids. They were his property and he should have been able to do whatever he wanted with them. They don't need schooling; they would never amount to anything anyway. They were supposed to work the farm, like he did when he was a boy.

His thoughts then drifted off to the latest property he had purchased. A potential buyer recently approached him, so he might not have to hang onto it for very long. *How many does that make now, five? Yep, five.*

Since he had arrived in Kansas, Charles had been buying up small farms and then reselling them. By holding the mortgages on them, his monthly income was growing. By far the largest purchase, his last property, would make for a good monthly payment. It wouldn't be long and he would own a lot of this county.

"Then I will start on the next county." Charles chuckled at the thought.

Yep, life was good and there was no stopping Charles Tuxhorn. He had more brains than the rest of his family put together. With Nettie by his side, he would build an empire that no one could touch.

The front screen door opened and the light of his life came out and handed him a drink.

CHAPTER TWENTY-FIVE

It had been a while since Charles bothered to go by the old house. It was winter and there wasn't much work to do except caring for the livestock. No planting or harvesting, so the work load lightened. Besides, he wanted to be close to Nettie, who was in her final weeks of pregnancy.

Most women wouldn't let a man touch her when she was with child, but not his Nettie. She wasn't a bit embarrassed as her stomach got big. She still stripped naked for him every night and let him listen to the sound of their baby's heartbeat or watch as the baby kicked from the inside out.

Nettie mesmerized Charles. Even while working, he seldom thought about anything else but her and her body. He actually had heard the heartbeat of his own kid. He never knew that was possible.

On December 9, 1903, Clarence F. Tuxhorn was born. Charles made sure the whole county knew about his son. He hired two women to clean the house and cook so Nettie could stay in bed for a few days and rest with their baby.

~~~

Things were getting desperate at the old house. Mary and Blaine couldn't get fruit or vegetables from the neighboring farms anymore. To make matters worse, it was turning out to be a very cold winter. It was also very difficult to cut wood for the stove to keep warm. That chore fell on Blaine, since he was the oldest boy. Only eleven, he didn't have the strength to swing an axe very hard. It would take hours after his chores to cut up enough for a fire.

One day, Charles came riding his horse out of the barn as Blaine was trying to cut pieces of wood for the stove. Blaine had not even known his poppa was in the barn. The child was having an awful time chopping wood, but he kept on trying. His father just rode past him as if he wasn't there. Not a glance or word to the boy as Blaine struggled with the big axe.

When his poppa was out of sight, Blaine sat down and cried. He wanted what everyone wanted, to be loved. Why didn't his poppa love him? Why did they have to live this way? Why did he have to chop all the wood? Why did they have to go hungry so much? After clearing his heart of some of the pain, he got up and continued to swing the axe. Only this time, he was aiming at his poppa's face when he hit the log.

Whatever they had to eat was consumed close to the stove for warmth. The oil for lamps ran out a month ago, so nights were long and dark. The children slept on the same old mattress to keep each other warm. Every blanket that Nettie didn't take to the new house was put on top of them. They would curl up under them and talk about their needs for survival. Sometimes Mary would hold Amos when he cried because he was hungry.

"Shush now, Amos. You are five now and big boys don't cry." Mary hated herself for using such a stupid cliché, but she didn't know what else to say. It broke her heart to see him cry.

"Why don't big boys cry, Momma?" Amos stopped crying and looked up at her with his big questioning eyes. The fact that he was now calling his sister "Momma" was a double-edged sword. One side of her heart melted that he loved her enough to call her momma; the other side broke because he will never know his real momma.

"They just don't. If anybody sees you cry, they will think you are still a baby. Now close your eyes and go to sleep. Tomorrow will be a better day." Mary could only hope her words would come true. But it seemed to appease Amos as he snuggled close to Mary and drifted off. Blaine smiled at her under the covers, then rolled over and covered Budge with his body so the boy would be warm.

~~~

Blaine and Budge were in school, and their lack of decent clothes and nourishment did not go unnoticed. The teacher would bring extra food in her own lunch. She would make a big deal out of being so silly to have brought too much, but didn't want it to go to waste.

"Why, I have done it again and packed too much and it will surely spoil if it isn't eaten."

Mrs. Carter was a sweet woman about thirty years old. With four children of her own, she couldn't imagine letting one of them starve. Two of her children were also in the same school. They knew what she was doing and why, but they never said a word, nor let anyone else in the school bring it up, either.

"Please help me out, Budge. Could you possibly find room in your tummy for this?"

Budge would look over at Blaine for guidance. Blaine gave a small nod and then, with that huge silly grin he said, "Yes, ma'am." Budge knew he wasn't too bright, but he began thinking his teacher wasn't either. She kept making the same mistake over and over. *Maybe she got hit in the head, too!*

There was no fooling Blaine, however, so she walked by his desk and dropped something on it. It always included a sandwich. Even if it was just a butter sandwich, it was something. He would take a bite or two and savor it, then put the rest went in his pocket to take home.

All the other kids knew about their terrible daddy. They had heard the grown-ups talk about some of the things he did to them. Children in school could be mean, and the boys were both teased about their clothes or if they missed a spelling word, but no one said a thing about the food. *That* would be cruel.

One afternoon when the school bell rang for everyone to go home, Blaine approached Mrs. Carter at her desk.

"Why do you do it?" Blaine asked.

"Do what, dear?" Mrs. Carter knew what he was asking, but she wanted him to keep as much pride as he could.

"You keep giving us food to eat. You don't do that for the others. Why do you do it?" Blaine didn't even know why he was asking. He had thought about it and knew he might be risking any future food to eat. Oh, he didn't care about himself, but he couldn't stand to see Budge or little Amos go without.

"Blaine, I am getting old and so forgetful. You know I have children to pack lunches for. Guess I just think I should add more in case I didn't pack them enough. Who knows what an old woman will do. But I sure do appreciate you and Budge helping me out, 'cause I don't want to hear the teasing I would get if I had to take that food home. Then they would all know what an idiot I really am." Mrs. Carter was doing her very best to look and sound sincere. She just couldn't stand the idea of humiliating this boy over something that was not his fault.

"Okay." Blaine looked at the floor for a moment.

Mrs. Carter remembered little Amos. Since Mary didn't come to school any more, the teacher had not seen him. He was old enough to start school next year on his own.

"Amos will start school in the fall, Blaine. How is he doing?" Mrs. Carter's heart skipped a little beat at that moment. *Please, Lord, don't let him be hurt by that monster he has for a father,* she thought to herself.

"He's fine, ma'am. Mary takes good care of him." Blaine didn't offer any more information.

Mrs. Carter was so glad to hear Amos was all right. All the kids were polite and nice looking, but that little Amos was a darling with his big blue eyes and rosy cheeks. *Just wait until he starts in the fall; I will be bringing twice as much food to eat!*

Blaine walked to the schoolroom door. Budge would be outside waiting so they could walk home together. When he reached the door, he stopped and turned back to his teacher.

MURDER IS A FAMILY AFFAIR

Looking her right in the eye, he said, "Thanks." It was a perfect case of 'she knew he knew' and 'he knew she knew he knew.'

Then he quickly added, "...And you're not old," and ran out the door. Mrs. Carter actually thought she felt a blush come on. Thinking about Blaine, she smiled. How could such a wonderful boy be the son of such a...

Well, some children do take after their mothers. Hmm, maybe mine will too. She laughed aloud at her own little joke.

~~~

About twice a month, firewood started showing up outside the old house. Not a lot, but enough to ensure they wouldn't freeze. It was a small-enough amount that Charles would not question it, if he saw it. The thought that anyone was helping them would get them all beaten. However, with his new baby here, they didn't have to worry about his showing up very often.

The new guardian angel was a mystery the children could never solve. Not at any time did they hear or see anyone near the house. Mary knew it had to be coming in the middle of the night, because when they were up and awake, there was no way anyone could get that close and not be seen or heard.

They suspected Frank Gamm, but he kept denying he had any part in it. Gamm said he was glad to hear the good news and, frankly, wished he had thought of it himself. But he said the Lord was using each person for His Will. But who could it be?

238

"You think it could be Uncle Leo bringing the wood?" Blaine was talking with his sister one night sitting in front of a new fire. The wind outside was howling and the temperatures had to be close to zero. It was the coldest winter they had experienced so far.

Mary had Amos on her lap and both were wrapped in a blanket. Budge and Blaine wrapped themselves together as well.

"You know we haven't seen him in a year. He doesn't care about us and neither does our granny. It just can't be him." Mary knew her uncle would probably help, even if grudgingly, if he knew they were in this bad of shape, but how would he ever know? Their poppa wasn't going to tell him. Their grandmother hardly acknowledged they existed, but everyone knew she was mean as dirt anyway, so it was just as well.

"I think it's Gamm," Budge chimed in, which he didn't often do. His brain didn't work as fast as it should after his poppa hit him in the head. When the older kids talked, Budge and Amos mostly listened. Budge's comment made Blaine and Mary laugh. It was just such a surprise to hear Budge jump into the conversation. He blushed and became quiet again.

"What we got for food tomorrow, Mary?" Blaine was almost afraid to hear the answer.

"At this point, Blaine, it is whatever you bring home from school." She hated to be blunt, but there it was.

They were quiet after that and sat in front of the fire until it was just dying embers, then they snuggled onto the old mattress. Before falling into an exhausted sleep, Mary wondered if they would actually live through the winter. Sometimes she didn't even care; at least, not about herself. She wouldn't want any harm coming to the others though. Her maturing motherly instincts kept her caring for her little brothers.

So, young lady, Mary thought as her mind was shutting down for the night, *guess I have to stick around to see these boys raised, somehow.*

As the days became shorter and colder, it seemed the more their guardian angel helped to keep them alive. Along with wood, one morning they found two bags of food—one was beans and the other rice. Mary started crying, in relief mostly, but also for having a lot of pressure removed from her small shoulders.

For the next month, they ate the rice and beans. Never once did anyone complain about eating the same thing day after day. They *had* something to eat and that was what counted. Once, a small hunk of beef showed up. They thought they were living like kings to have meat on the table. Mary cooked it all and dished out portions of the beef over five days. Their poppa never brought food anymore, so they knew they had a guardian angel.

~~~

It was around the first week of February, 1904, when the school day was over and all the children had gone home that a man limped into the schoolroom on a cane. Mrs. Carter looked up and smiled.

"How's everything going, ma'am?" The man asked, looking around to make sure no one was watching.

"Well, everything seems fine. Budge tells me the children have been eating beans and rice these days, even a little meat. That is such a sweet child. He will never be quite right, but he sure is adorable. It also seems they have been able to build a fire at night to keep warm."

"That's good, with this weather and all." The man hesitated a bit, then came to the point. "What more do they need, Mrs. Carter?"

She got up from her desk, passed the man, and went to shut her classroom door so they could talk privately.

Walking back to him, she said, "Mostly they need love, John, but in lieu of that, they need what you are supplying— food to eat and wood to keep warm. I don't know how you are doing it without their knowledge, but I do know God is in Heaven watching the wonderful things you are doing for those children."

"It ain't much, I know. I would drop off enough to keep them for the whole winter, but I know Tuxhorn would kill them for accepting it." John hesitated and looked down at his damaged leg. "And then he would kill me for giving it."

John Friesen turned and quietly hobbled out of the schoolroom. He just couldn't get away from the heavy burden on his shoulders. His own daughter was responsible for those children being left to die. What kind of person had he raised?

"Lord God, please forgive, me but I have a big problem here." John was thinking aloud as he headed his buggy home from the school. "I just can't forgive her. I just can't. How could she become this wanton woman who takes up with the most evil man I have ever met? How can she sit in her nice new house and not care what happens to all those little children?"

There were too many questions and no answers. The one thing he did know for sure was the children could never know what he was doing. He couldn't chance the outcome with Tuxhorn. He could not be responsible for getting any one of them kids hurt.

He pulled his coat collar up over his neck. It was another cold one. He was glad he had dropped off some wood for the children two days before, because this getting up in the middle of the night to sneak out of the house and quietly drop things off was getting to him. Only his wife knew what was going on, because he couldn't chance one of his own kids saying anything to Blaine or Budge in school.

"I am getting too old for this, Lord!" Just hearing himself say it aloud made him chuckle. *One day at a time John*, he seemed to hear the Lord say in his heart. *Get the children through the winter.*

When he walked into his house, his wife looked up with a question on her face. He knew what she wanted to know.

"Everything's fine. Everything's fine—for now." It was really the only thing he could say. His wife smiled.

~~~

Mrs. Friesen made sure the next drop off included new clothes to replace the battered ones. She made them at night when her children were asleep so they would not find out. She used different material for coats and tops so her own children would not recognize anything she made. It cost some sleep, but nothing was too high a price to pay for the peace in her heart. God would have expected no less of her.

John could be stubborn sometimes, she knew that. But in this case, she had to agree with him. Nettie being involved with the negligence of those children was beyond her understanding, and, like her husband, try as she might, she couldn't forgive her. Nettie's name was not to be mentioned in their home again. Because of the shame she brought to the Friesen family, it was their duty to help those children. And, God forgive her, if that meant upsetting that Tuxhorn devil, then so be it.

CHAPTER TWENTY-SIX

Charles' reputation for an out-of-control temper was always fodder for gossip in the county. It certainly wasn't getting any better with age. Apparently it was never aimed at Nettie, but she had to be aware of it. As sheriff, at least he didn't have to worry about that, too.

Getting into a fight with someone in town, however, was almost a regular event for him. It didn't take much for someone to set ol' Charles off and that usually meant someone would need a doctor. Even when the fight included two or three against him, his uncontrollable temper would provide the adrenaline needed to take them on. Then it would take another two or three men to pull him off the poor suckers.

It was nearly impossible to charge Charles with a crime when he had three men on him. Other times, when he questioned them, no one would say Charles swung first, whether he did or not. They knew Tuxhorn would come after them if they made accusations. It was better left alone. When it came to Tuxhorn, it was frustrating being the sheriff. Very frustrating.

Those momentarily brave enough to speak against Charles would sometimes find themselves mugged at night, but never able to identify their attacker. A couple men didn't live long enough to even try. The sheriff knew it was Tuxhorn, but no one could prove it. Prove it or not, it was a foolish man who wasn't afraid of Charles Tuxhorn.

He kept most people talking, but street and barroom brawls were nothing like the time that poor ol' preacher man came into town. It supplied gossip for weeks.

One morning, Charles rode into town and swung off his horse in front of the mercantile. Just as he was tying up, the preacher came up behind him. Not knowing Charles or his reputation, he wanted to make friends with the stranger. As sheriff, he only heard about this later from town folk, because he was still in his office at the time.

"Hello, friend. My name is Johnson Thomas Chesterfield. I know it is an odd name, but you can just call me J.T.; all my friends do. I am a preacher traveling to Arizona to do God's work. I'll be in town a little while and would sure like to see you at the prayer meeting Sunday."

Somehow he managed to say all this without taking a second breath. J.T. stuck his right hand out for Charles to shake when he turned around. The preacher was grinning from ear to ear.

Though physically about the same size as Charles, J.T. wore eyeglasses and had a goofy grin. His full beard had a touch of grey in it that told him to be about forty-something

246

years old. His clothes were cheap and he carried a large bible in his left hand, with dog-eared pages.

People immediately around the two stopped dead in their tracks. Fear filled the air. It was too late to get the good preacher out of the way. A couple of men stood ready just in case they had to try and save the poor guy.

Hearing the voice behind him apparently caused Charles to bristle. Everyone knew he hated strangers accosting him. He hated it as much as he did when people he *knew* accosted him. But nothing, nothing, could compare to how much he hated preachers.

The sheriff was told Charles turned around very slowly and looked the man squarely in the eye. Then he slowly looked him up and down. The silence was palatable. The widow Baker even started to cry.

Within a split second, Charles grabbed that extended hand and twisted it behind the preacher's back, holding him in a headlock. When he spoke into the preacher's ear, J.T. said he could hear the evil swimming in his voice.

"I don't care who you are, you filthy pig, and I am *not* your friend. If you ever speak to me again, I will feed what is left of you to the coyotes. Do you hear me?"

Charles' voice was low. "All you preachers are worthless. Do you really think you can shove that garbage down my throat and expect me to dance to it? *Do* you?"

"Noooo, sir. Sorry if I bothered you, sir." J.T.'s voice was choked with fear as much as the pressure of the arm across his windpipe. He ran into mean people from time to time, those who didn't think they needed salvation, but this one seemed different. This fellow's hatred was deep and he meant every word. And J.T. told the sheriff later, that he knew it.

Still in his office, Sheriff Gleason got restless and decided to step out of his office. As soon as he did, he saw everyone had stopped in their tracks looking at someone. That someone was Charles Tuxhorn.

Charles saw the sheriff step outside his office. He knew the slightest provocation was all he would need to arrest him. *Anything. Just give him anything.*

Charles quickly released his grip around the neck, spun the man back around to face him, and, still holding his right hand, pretended to be shaking it. It turned out his grip broke two of the preacher's fingers.

"Well, nice to meet you, J.T. Have a nice day," Charles said.

Gleason knew it was for his benefit. Charles had a big smile on this face and the comment was loud enough for everyone to hear. He then got on his horse and rode out of town.

The townspeople surrounded poor J.T., as the sheriff caught up to him. With his fingers in a lot of pain, he was pretty shook up. Folks informed him not to get in Tuxhorn's way again and he now believed it was good advice.

The talk of Charles mistreating a man of God was one that everyone in the county heard eventually; most heard it many times.

The sheriff kept hounding the preacher to file charges against Tuxhorn for breaking his fingers, but the preacher would have none of it. He didn't want to incur the wrath of the devil again, and no one could blame him. He looked into those blue eyes, like they all had, and knew there was no redemption. No, sir. He wasn't going to say a bad word against

Charles Tuxhorn. It was okay if he didn't ever lay eyes upon him again. But then they all felt that way, too.

"I am a man of God, Sheriff Gleason." The preacher almost stuttered, still shaking with fear. It was the only explanation he could come up with that would keep him from looking like a coward. "I am supposed to forgive and forget. I won't be here that long, anyway. I won't do it."

What does it take to get Tuxhorn? The sheriff got mighty frustrated just thinking about it. The man was a terror to everyone. No one was exempt from his temper. What was it going to take to stop him? A bullet between his eyes would help, and he would sure be pleased if it was one of his. Badgering the poor preacher was not going to get anywhere, so the sheriff left him alone.

Gossip about this confrontation just wouldn't go away. Tales of Tuxhorn coming after the preacher circulated for days. Two weeks later when the preacher finally left for Arizona, the rumors changed from his demise to the sheriff's.

One had him sneaking into town in the middle of the night and slashing his throat while he slept. The sheriff had to admit, some of their blabbering got under his skin.

"You know, ol' Tuxhorn is gonna stop that sheriff in his dreams! One night he won't wake up, that's for sure!" Stupid people.

A couple of weeks after his encounter with the preacher, old Gladys Matthews swore she saw Tuxhorn having a polite conversation with the preacher behind the stables in town. She said they looked down right friendly. She even said Mr. Tuxhorn looked up, and when he saw her watching them, he waved. Of course, scared out of her mind, she moved on quickly at that point. That one brought laughter as well as unending jokes about her taking too much of that tonic she used for her headaches.

One day, Sheriff Gleason walked into the saloon for an afternoon drink. Those already there decided to have some fun at his expense.

"Hey, Sheriff! I saw that preacher fellow and Tuxhorn walking down the road smiling at each other. I hear Tuxhorn will be in church this coming Sunday." The old livery man was on his 'one too many' drinks at the saloon.

"Sure, Jake. Lay off the liquor for a while, will you? You know your wife will come in here with that broom of hers and beat us all up for letting you get drunk." The sheriff got his own round of laughter for that one.

"Sheriff!" Another patron chimed in. "I heard Tuxhorn was dying to be your best friend...or was that he just wanted you dying!" Bret Sampson was yelling from a side table. Laughter rang out again.

Smiling at their ribbing, the sheriff swallowed his drink, shook his head and walked back out into the sunlight. *Booze made idiots out of...well, come to think of it, they were idiots sober.* Gleason laughed out loud at the thought and went back to his office.

~~~

Winter, fighting to stay for every frigid breath, finally relinquished possession of the land to spring. The longer days of farming started again for everyone.

From April on, school ended for Blaine. Budge attended with Amos. Mrs. Carter was used to children not showing up during planting or harvesting. That was just the way it was.

Mary and Blaine had to work the farm during the day. The work was hard and days were long. One of their responsibilities was to round up the cows, making sure they came home and were fenced in. When Budge and Amos got out of school, they went home to do their part. Spring finally gave way to summer and they all were out of school. It was not much of a childhood, but they still had each other.

"Blaine," Mary started a conversation she had been thinking about for a couple of months. It was now about the middle of summer and they had to make a decision. "I have something I want to talk to you about."

"Sure, Mary." Blaine's ears perked up because he knew the tone in her voice meant she was serious. Did they have another problem? It was summer again and they had fresh food to eat, so it couldn't be too serious. Nothing was more serious than that.

"Blaine, I don't know if we can survive another winter like the last." She wanted to start out slowly.

"It was hard, no doubt." Blaine was musing over some of the worse times. "But we made it okay, didn't we, Mary?"

"Yes, but it was by the Grace of God Himself and the help of some unknown person that we did." Mary still tried to figure out who helped with food, wood, and then some much-needed clothes.

"But what if the person who helped us leaves town or can't help us next winter? We found out we can't do it ourselves."

"So, what are you thinking, Mary?" Blaine wasn't following her drift. He didn't see any alternatives.

"Blaine, we have to get out of here. We gotta get out like Bertha, Tilly, and Edward did. We will surely die if we don't. Poppa will kill us or the weather will; either way, we will never make it." Mary had finally said what she had been thinking for so long. She had often wondered what Blaine would think and now she was going to find out.

"Well..." Blaine started out slowly while he tried to wrap his brain around her statement. "Where would we go and how would we get there?"

"I don't know. To some relative, I guess. I don't have it worked out yet, but we have to do something before winter sets in again." Mary knew she had to work out the plan and pick a good time.

"Oh, Mary," Blaine said. "I don't think anything is going to happen to us. Poppa doesn't come around much anymore. I think we'll be all right."

Well, Mary had to bring it up. She still felt uneasy about it all. She couldn't believe Blaine would have that much faith in their ability to survive after all they went through last winter. Nevertheless, Mary knew from the expression on his face that the seed had been planted. Her brother's mind was turning it all over.

Time, however, moved faster than summer lightning. Longer daylight hours meant more working time. The month of August brought harvest along with it. They got up exhausted and went to bed exhausted.

Mary was starting to mature physically and Blaine was growing tall. At twelve, he was a good two inches above Mary and she was proud of the man he was becoming. Budge, too, was growing taller, and she was pleased whoever had made the clothes left a lot of hem for letting them out.

Before they had time to take a breath, school was starting again. Mary was about to turn fourteen. Blaine was twelve and his two siblings were going on nine and six. For the next few months, Mary and Blaine talked about the possibilities of leaving after they put the young ones ~~went~~ to bed.

"Winter is coming, Blaine. We have to figure out what to do." Mary knew they would be in trouble if they waited much longer.

"I know. What if we went to live with Uncle Leo?" Blaine knew he was grasping at straws.

"Forget it. Uncle Leo would never do it and Poppa would never allow it. We have to get as far away as possible." Mary had already thought through the possibility of Uncle Leo and knew it was a dead end.

"We would have to walk, but if we stayed off the main roads, we could stay hidden." Blaine's mind was now dealing with the issue.

"I know. We would just walk until we found somewhere to stop. That's all we can do." Mary didn't have solid answers either, but she was glad Blaine was finally willing to talk about it.

"What about Budge and Amos? They are still young, especially Amos. How would we make it with them?" Blaine had a very good point, but Mary didn't want to hear it.

"I don't know." Mary sighed. "We just would. We would have to go slower, but we would be all right."

Good intentions fell behind farm work and school. It wasn't much of a life, but it certainly flew by quickly.

The first week in November, an early snowstorm proved they had waited too long. They were stuck for another winter, and Mary knew they were in for a tough time.

CHAPTER TWENTY-SEVEN

It wasn't starvation that would seal their fate that winter, as Mary assumed. John Friesen kept coming over in the middle of the night, but this winter he had the help of his oldest son to make sure everything was carried out as planned. John wasn't able to do it alone anymore, and his oldest had been sworn to secrecy.

Mrs. Friesen made each child a set of clothes for winter, including coats. She intentionally made them to be a little larger than she thought they might need, to help them get through the year. She had been told how tall Blaine was growing and that Mary's body was filling out. The coats being so comfortable and warm, the children would even sleep in them, when the cold was too much.

It was a cold Sunday afternoon in late December when their tenuous world finally fell apart. Blaine made a simple error. After getting all of the cows gathered for the night, somehow the gate came open and they got out. Blaine ran into the house screaming for Mary.

"Help, Mary, the cows are out!" Blaine could hardly breathe.

"Noooooo! Blain, we'll get killed. Come on, let's go, Budge!" Mary's mind was racing while she put on her coat. Budge didn't question her demand. Blaine quickly hooked a makeshift leash to Amos and the cook stove, so he couldn't leave the house and freeze to death while they worked. Then he ran after Mary and Budge.

The three began the nightmare roundup. They walked miles to find each one. Most of them had wandered onto Frank Gamm's place to the north, and he helped the children get them headed back in the right direction. However, he did not pass over his neighbor's property line. He knew Charles would use that as a legal excuse to shoot him for trespassing.

It took hours to find and get them all back. When the last one was in and the gate shut solid, if was well after dark. Standing outside the pen, Mary finally broke down and cried.

"Don't cry, Mary. We got 'em back, every one of 'em." They were all exhausted and Blaine didn't like to see Mary upset. Glancing over at his brother, nine-year-old Budge looked too tired to even make it home.

"Getting them back is not the point, Blaine. Poppa will kill us. He will blame us for them getting out in the first place." She was wiping at her tears as they walked toward their house when the nightmare became real.

Charles Tuxhorn rode his horse out of the dark, right in front of them. Three little hearts skipped a beat in fear while their bodies stood at attention, staring straight ahead, not daring to even look at Charles.

"All of you are worthless. No better than pig slime. I don't know why I even put up with you. You let those cows out today and they could have been stolen. What were you trying to do, get Frank Gamm to take our beef? You will *pay* for this, you can bet on it." Charles was outraged, and leaning down from the saddle, practically spat in her face as Mary stood frozen.

"I'm going to McPherson for a few days, but when I get back, all of you are going to get what you have coming. Do you hear me? You are going to pay *dearly*." Charles turned his horse and galloped away into the dark.

The three of them stood where they were, hearing him ride off, afraid to turn in his direction. Then, almost as if a signal had been sounded, they all started running for their house. With the door slammed and locked behind them, Mary grabbed little Amos and held him tight while Blaine started a fire. She thought of nothing more than the look on Poppa's face. What did they do to make him hate them so much? She was too scared now to even cry.

"Blaine, we are in a lot of trouble. Poppa's gonna beat us bad when he gets back." Amos started to cry when he heard what she said. "Hush, Amos." She wrapped him in her blanket tighter.

Blaine looked like it was his turn to cry. Choking back the tears, he agreed. "You're right, Mary. What are we gonna do? He will kill us this time for sure!"

"We'll talk about it later." Mary was in mother mode again. She got them all a little something to eat, and then tucked Amos and Budge into bed. She motioned for Blaine to meet her by the fire.

"We have to run away. Now. Poppa will be gone a few days, and we have to leave before he gets back." Mary knew there was no other choice.

"Mary, it is December! We will have to walk and Amos will freeze to death." Blaine had put her thoughts into words.

"I know. We can't take Amos. He will not be blamed for the cows like we will. We will take Amos to school in the morning and then we will leave." Mary knew this is what they had to do, but the thought of leaving Amos struck a pain through her heart. None of them would make it in the snow if they didn't leave him behind. She knew it, but she didn't have to like it.

Mary packed up a little for each to carry and what little food was left. Come morning, they took Amos to school. Each one kissed him goodbye and told him when he got out of school for him to go to Poppa's new house to stay.

They went to Uncle Leo's house, where he made them dinner. Before they left, Blaine asked for money to travel on. He refused, not wanting to get involved in the problems of others. They begged and told him their poppa would beat them to death if they stayed. He finally relented and gave them $1.80.

That was it. Mary, Blaine, and Budge started walking east, staying off the main roads and curling up together in a ball at night to stay warm.

Hearing of their plight, local people put together some money and bought them tickets to Fort Scott, Kansas. It was there Mary believed an uncle lived. For the first time, the three actually thought they had a chance to get free. Fate would soon dash their hopes.

Upon their arrival in Fort Scott, they quickly discovered their uncle had moved away. They were so disappointed. Now they would have to find somewhere else to go. Once again, walking was the only way to get there.

This put the three on the course to Mulberry, Missouri, where another uncle lived. The distance was fifty miles, and they walked every step of the way. There was no food to eat except what they could find. On one particular day, they lived on walnuts alone. Mulberry, Missouri, was a welcome sight.

"We made it! We actually made it." Mary knew they had no choice but to leave home, but actually having accomplished the escape was almost more than she could comprehend.

"We're free, Mary. We can live without fear of poppa." Blaine was exhausted but happy to have escaped the cruelty.

They soon found out their uncle had passed on; however they were welcomed by his widow.

The three of them cried constantly for little Amos. They had made their escape, but at what cost? How they missed him. None of them could bear the fact he was in his poppa's house.

~~~

December had rolled into January of 1905. Blaine found a job husking corn, staying in the employer's bunkhouse. Mary and Budge stayed with their aunt. The stories of the cruelty against all the children spread like wildfire. Some even went to the sheriff of Bates County, where they were, which caused the law to investigate.

After talking with the children and seeing the marks of abuse on their bodies, the law decided to step in and stop the horror. This led to the arrest of Charles Tuxhorn for child abuse on Friday, January 6, 1905.

If there was ever a job that made Sheriff Gleason smile, it was this one. When he received the telegram from the Bates County sheriff, he felt it was a sign from the Almighty that He wasn't going to take any more from that evil man.

How did that telegram put it? "There is sufficient evidence to arrest Charles H. Tuxhorn for cruelty to his children." How beautiful those words sounded to him.

Late that Friday, Sheriff Gleason gathered four of his best, armed deputies to ride out to the Tuxhorn farm. He had planned it to be after dark so Charles would be home and likely unarmed, which is exactly how they found him.

Hearing the knock on the door, Charles opened it to find five men standing in front of him with guns drawn. They were ready to shoot for any reason. It wasn't thirty seconds later that he was arrested and handcuffed. Nettie stood in the living room watching, unable to do or say anything.

"Don't worry, honey, I'll be back in the morning. I love you." Charles was joking as if he had planned this himself.

Gleason knew, however, that inside he was mortified and furious that he was arrested in front of his wife.

The sheriff couldn't have been more delighted. For the law to interfere in a man's domestic problems required the claims to be severely life threatening; after all, it was 1905, not the dark ages. In the case of Charles Tuxhorn, Sheriff Gleason knew the children had the wounds and scars to prove the truth of their statements.

Incarcerated for three days, Charles bonded out for fifteen hundred dollars. His trial was set for Monday, January 23, 1905, approximately two weeks later.

Gleason made the trip to Missouri to bring the children back to testify in court against their father. He had arranged a safe place for them to stay prior to court.

"Sheriff, I don't understand." Mary said while packing up to leave Missouri.

"Why isn't Budge coming back with us?" Blaine stated the very thought that had crossed Mary's mind.

"Kids, Budge is too young. He's only nine years old. Plus, he wouldn't make a good witness, and you know that. By leaving him here, he will be safe and won't have to come back." It made perfect sense to the sheriff and would make the trip back a whole lot easier not having another kid to take care of, especially one that seemed a bit off in the head. He didn't need any more trouble than he already had.

Mary and Blaine finally agreed that it made sense and said their goodbyes to Budge. The Sheriff told the aunt that someone would come for him shortly. What "shortly" meant, he didn't explain. Nor did he say who would be coming for him.

When a few days passed, with no further word about picking up the child, the aunt sent a telegraph to inquire. She sent it to the child's father, Charles Tuxhorn.

After receiving the telegraph, letting him know where Budge was, he immediately went to Missouri to pick him up. When he was again back in McPherson County, now having custody of his two youngest boys, he demanded the return

261

of his two other children. This request was denied by the court. But the fact that Charles now had Amos and Budge was devastating news.

Blaine and Mary pleaded with the sheriff to go get them both away from their poppa, as it was too dangerous.

"Please, Sheriff, *please* go get Amos and Budge from poppa. He's gonna beat them near to death if you don't." Blaine was shedding as many tears as Mary. They had been like parents to those little boys and couldn't stand the thought they might be in harm's way. The pain in their hearts consumed them.

Sheriff Gleason couldn't understand the hysterics of these two children. They wouldn't let up! They were begging him to pick up the little boys. Why did they cry so?

"Don't you worry, kids. Your poppa isn't going to harm them boys, not with these charges against him. I expect he will take real good care of them." Sheriff Gleason wanted to calm their fears.

Tuxhorn wasn't stupid. These charges were serious and he wasn't going to add to them. Sheriff Gleason knew that. He had to calm Mary and Blaine down. It would all be over in just a few more days.

A violent-natured man arrested for child abuse might result in unusual conduct. However, it produced an effect on Charles Tuxhorn that no one could have guessed. He turned nice. Really nice.

~~~

Charles spent a lot of time in town, smiling and joking with everyone. He told tales how his children had done *him* wrong. To all who would stop and listen, he showed destroyed clothes that the kids were supposed to have cut to ribbons. No one believed such tales.

He ordered two new shotguns from Montgomery Ward and paid express delivery. Charles told everyone they were for his sons to go hunting with him. Townspeople also knew that not to be true. Charles wouldn't even feed his children, let alone give them something they could use to protect themselves—especially from their own father.

The whole town was uneasy. Charles spent a lot of time every day talking with anyone who would listen about what a good father he was. He would smile and make jokes about how patient he had been with them, and this was how they paid him back.

On January 17, 1905, Charles went to the closest big city, Hutchinson, Kansas, to hire a high-powered lawyer. F.P. Hettinger, Esquire, to be exact.

Hettinger held the distinct title of the most powerful attorney in Hutchinson. A pillar of society, he and his family dominated the social scene. His services weren't cheap, by any means. Charles knew money was no object when you needed the best, and the best was what he needed now.

A male secretary escorted Charles into Hettinger's office and sat him in a large comfortable leather chair. The desk in front of him was huge. He had never seen anything like it. The whole office spoke "old money," and lots of it.

The attorney came into the office from a side door, not the one Charles came through. He was tall, white-headed, and perfectly dressed. Charles could see the impressive appearance he would make in court. For a moment, he was glad to be here.

"I have looked over the charges, Mr. Tuxhorn, as well as the evidence."

Indeed, he had read the sheriff's reports and reviewed the sketches of the marks on the children's bodies. From what he already knew, Hettinger didn't like the man in front of his desk and wanted to get this meeting over with.

There was no doubt in his mind the man was vile. A lawyer for over thirty years, however, he would never let his personal feelings show on his face.

"Yes sir," Charles said trying to appear humble. "They are all lies. The sheriff stole my children and has told them what to say to discredit me."

"The evidence seems real. Mary and Blaine have scars and injuries to prove it." Hettinger did not like this case at all. He stared right at Tuxhorn to see his response.

"They are always clumsy—falling, cutting themselves. They take after their mother that way. She was stupid and clumsy, too. It wasn't me." Charles threw out anything he could.

"Well, Mr. Tuxhorn, you have hired me for my advice, and this is it. It is apparent to me, from a strictly legal point of view…" Hettinger wanted to make that clear. As his attorney, Tuxhorn's guilt or innocence was not for him to say.

"…they have the charges and the evidence they need to convict you." As an attorney, he hastened to add, "I am not saying you are guilty of any wrongdoing, merely what will appear to be the truth to the court."

F.P. Hettinger continued. "I probably will not be able to help much to combat the evidence. However, I will do my best to see if we can obtain as short a sentence as possible."

His final legal advice for Charles, "You will need to get your affairs in order, Mr. Tuxhorn. You will most likely be going to jail for a while. Your court date is for Monday, January twenty-third. Be in my McPherson office at 7 A.M., and we will go to court together."

They both stood. "Yes, sir. Thank you, sir. You have told me what I needed to know." Charles smiled, and shook the attorney's outstretched hand, and left.

Mr. Hettinger had indeed given him the information he needed. Charles had formulated a plan and it was time to put it in motion. It would be hard to get everything done in the six days remaining before trial, but he would have to make it work.

There was one more stop to make while in town. He went to the druggist and asked for Dr. Davis' Headache Powder. The pharmacist smiled and nodded.

"You have bad headaches, sir?" the man behind the counter asked.

"Yes, I do. The only thing that will work for me is Dr. Davis' Headache Powder. Nothing else will help me," Charles said.

"You don't have any trouble with it? Some folks say it is too strong." The man was happy to hear his customer was doing fine with this product.

"No problems, sir. In fact, since I don't get here too often, I will take two bottles." Charles mind was mostly elsewhere, but he needed to get this done so he could get home.

"Here you go. Thanks for coming in."

Charles headed home to implement his newly formed plans.

CHAPTER TWENTY-EIGHT

U pon arriving home from his trip to see Mr. Hettinger, Charles put a sign in his yard and an ad in the paper. Everything he had was up for sale, except his own farm.

Within a few days, he sold all of his equipment, livestock, and horses. In answer to their questions, Charles told everyone he was getting ready for his time in prison. He had to liquidate to take care of his wife.

Gathering the mortgages held on other farms and the cash made from sales, he took it all to the bank and traded them for gold. It was Eleven thousand dollars in gold, to be exact. It was more money than most saw in a lifetime, but it was not all of Charles' assets.

Since arriving from Missouri with over twenty-five thousand dollars in gold, he had kept a stash buried under the floor of his house in gas pipe receptacles he had made. He then put those in a milk can that fit in a hole under the house.

No one really knew how much money was left in the buried milk can or whether any had been buried elsewhere on the property. One thing that was known was Charles had a lot of gold, an estimated massive fortune of $30,000 all told.

Having liquidated all his assets, he changed the farm over into Nettie's name. None of his children from his previous marriage were to have anything of his. He made sure of that. He told all who would listen he was making sure his wife was taken care of while he was gone away to prison. People were amazed and he was, as usual, the talk of the town. The most astonishing thing of all, this was all accomplished in a mere three days.

During Friday evening, January 20, 1905, Charles sat down and wrote three letters, which he sealed in envelopes. It was time to sit Nettie down and let her know she would be leaving in the morning.

"Nettie, darling, I love you. You are good and you have my heart. But our time together is over." Charles was having a tough time thinking about a future without Nettie, but there was no longer a choice.

"Charles, I don't know what you are saying." Nettie had been in a state of confusion for the past week. The arrest, the attorney, selling everything—it was all happening too fast. What was she going to do without her husband?

"Nettie, tomorrow is Saturday and I am going to pack you and our baby, Clarence, into the buggy and send you off to your sister's. Don't worry, there is plenty of money, and you will not go without." Charles wanted her to know he would take care of her.

"I will be taking the boys with me to McPherson to be there for the trial starting Monday morning. You stay with your sister until it is safe to come home." Charles didn't know any other way to put it.

"Safe? Why wouldn't it be safe here? Charles?" Nettie was more confused than ever. Why would it not be safe to stay in their own home?

"Just do as I say, Nettie. It will all work out for the best." Charles stood and kissed his wife on the forehead and walked away.

The conversation was over, but the planning was not. He still had a lot to do. Leaving the house, he told Nettie not to wait up for him, as he would be busy most of the night.

The following morning, Nettie fixed breakfast then cleaned the kitchen. As he requested, she sewed a button onto Charles' pants and put away some clean laundry. She then set about packing for herself and her son, Clarence. She didn't pay any attention to Amos and Budge, who had been living with them for the past two or three weeks. They were not her responsibility, and they had to go with their father to court anyway.

About three in the afternoon, Nettie, nicely dressed and sporting a new bonnet, was ready to leave. Charles brought the buggy around with two horses he hadn't sold, because they were Nettie's favorites. The only horse left was an old one tethered way out in a pasture.

Before she climbed aboard, Charles kissed the only woman he had ever loved. After she was seated, he picked up thirteen-month-old Clarence and hugged him tightly.

"Take good care of your momma, little man. I'm counting on you." Charles never knew he could have feelings for a child before. Clarence giggled as he was lifted up to his mother who then sat him down in the buggy beside her.

"Goodbye, Nettie. No matter what happens, just remember I love you." Charles let her go and watched the buggy turn onto the county road. He wondered why he had to lose the only thing in life he had ever really wanted. As Nettie rode away, there was the very beginning of new life in her womb, which would produce twin girls for Charles, exactly nine months later.

When Blaine and Mary heard that Nettie left for her sister's house, they once again became hysterical. Repeatedly, they begged the sheriff to remove Budge and Amos from their father. They were alone with him now and he would hurt them.

"Please! Please! Bring them into town. I will watch them, sheriff. I always have. PLEASE!" Mary was past hysterics. Her heart hurt for her little brothers and she hadn't seen Amos since she left him in school the day they had to leave without him.

"She's right, sir. Please go get them!" Blaine, too, was crying so hard he could hardly breathe. "We're *begging* you!"

The sheriff just wanted this whole thing to be over. "Kids, please! Everything will be all right. The trial starts in two days. He won't be a threat to you any longer. You will all be back together in such a short time, so stop worrying about it. You will see them on Monday. Now, don't ask again!"

That was that. The sheriff didn't want to deal with it any more. It was obvious their hearts were breaking, but there was nothing he could do about it before Monday. Mary and Blaine held each other and cried for hours.

~~~

Nettie and the baby were in town now, where they would be safe. Charles was ready to continue with his plan.

He returned to the new house and proceeded to dress Amos and Budge into new dress clothes. He had purchased the clothes for them in order to impress the court that he was a good father. The new clothes would have a better use now than Charles first imagined.

"Come on, boys. Let's go watch the world go by." Charles headed for the front door with the little ones right behind him. He grabbed a chair off the porch and they all walked toward the road. It was just cold enough to maintain the patches of snow that still clung to the ground here and there. Otherwise, the sun was shining and quite pleasant.

Charles put his chair right in the middle of the property entrance and sat down. The boys were confused and curious, but not frightened. In their short lives, nothing their father did was to be questioned, so neither one of them asked why they were standing there.

They were wearing better clothes than they had ever had in their entire lives. They thought they looked great all dressed up, and their poppa was treating them very nice;y. He had not said any bad words to them or anything. Mary and Blaine would never believe this when they told them. Amos picked up on Budge's contagious smile and both looked happy.

The three spent an hour or two during early evening saying hello to all who came down the county road. At one point, John Friesen was headed into town. When he saw Charles sitting by the road up ahead, he stopped his buggy, afraid to continue any farther.

John didn't remember most of his beating at Tuxhorn's hands, but he did remember the long recovery and the bum leg. What would he do to him now? Shaking his head a bit, he decided to ride on by. What happened next would be in God's hands.

No one could have been more surprised than John, when he heard, "Good afternoon, John. How ya doing?" Charles even sounded happy.

Leery of Charles' intentions, John pulled to a stop at the entrance to the Tuxhorn farm and answered him. "Fine, Charles. How 'bout yourself?"

John noticed the two boys were all dressed up and standing beside the chair their poppa sat in. He also noted the smiles on their faces. This was a scene out of a nightmare...a really bad nightmare.

"We are just fine. As you can see, my boys are here, Budge and Amos. We are just visiting with whomever wants to come by today." Charles smiled.

"Say, John, Nettie was of the opinion you wouldn't let her stay at your house anymore because she married me. Is that true?"

John instinctively panicked. He felt as if this was a trap. The last time the two of them spoke of Nettie, it almost cost him his life. He warned himself to be very careful of every word he said.

"Why, no, Charles. I don't know of any reason she can't stay with us." That was the only safe comment John could think to make, and he quickly said a little prayer asking God to forgive him for stretching the truth. He actually could think of a dozen reasons he didn't want her back in his house, but this was not the time to go into them.

"Well, that's good, John. Real good. She will need somewhere to stay while I'm in jail, you know. She rode into town earlier and is at her sister's house."

The whole encounter was almost more than John could bear. He felt ill and thought he would be sick to his stomach. Had Charles finally lost his mind, or was John, himself, hallucinating?

Charles had never said a nice word to him, had tried to kill him once, and now he wanted to pass the time of day? John shuddered at the sight in front of him. Lord, something just wasn't right here.

"Well, you all have a nice day." John couldn't wait to leave.

"Same to you, John. Have a nice day. Wave goodbye to Mr. Friesen, boys." All three waved as John rode off.

The encounter shook John so badly that he later confided in his wife that something was terribly wrong at the Tuxhorn farm. They immediately began to pray for guidance. God was the only One who could make sense of this now.

A brother-in-law from Nettie's family rode by and received a similar reception. Introducing the boys to him, Charles spoke about the weather.

"Have a nice day, now." Charles waved him goodbye. Everyone that came by left more scared of him than ever before.

It was after five in the evening and beginning to get dark when Charles stood, picked up his chair, and told the boys it was time to go back to the house. Once there, Charles set about making supper for them all, since Nettie wasn't there to cook. He said he would fix them a plate of beans and the boys thought that sounded great.

Budge set the table as Mary had taught him to do. It was six-thirty when they finally sat down to eat. Charles continued to talk to them as though they were his friends.

"We'll ride up to McPherson tomorrow. Then we can be up early for court on Monday." Charles was actually enjoying himself. "How do you like your new clothes?"

"I love them, Poppa," little Amos said, looking down at his jacket. Budge, as always, just grinned. Both loved being all dressed up.

Shortly after dinner, the boys weren't feeling well and asked if they could go lie down.

"That's fine. You go and take a nap until you feel better. But don't take off your good clothes; we have other things to do later." Charles watched them go to their bedroom.

He then set about cleaning up the food and dishes in the kitchen. He wiped down the table to make sure it was clean. He would need it later.

About an hour after they went to lie down, Charles went in to check on the boys. He was not happy with what he found. Both were unconscious, but, unfortunately, still alive.

The poison in their dinner was enough to kill a horse, or at least Charles thought it was. Recently discovered as toxic, the over-the-counter headache remedy, Dr. Davis' Headache Powder, was pure acetanilide, a deadly drug killing people all over the country.

Numerous products contained acetanilide and many were responsible for severe illnesses or death. However, none had the concentration of Dr. Davis' Headache Powder, which turned out to be almost 100% pure.

Some merchants were skeptical of the death reports filtering in and still sold it in their stores. Charles knew it would work well into his plans.

After separating his beans from theirs, he mixed one entire bottle into their dinner. He would have used the second bottle if Mary and Blaine had been present, but that didn't pan out quite right, thanks to that stupid sheriff. But, he'll deal with Gleason later tonight.

A grown man had reportedly died from one tablespoon of this headache powder, so he figured a whole bottle would take care of those children quickly. So why were they still breathing?

Each child suffered severely, as any poison victim would. Their internal organs shut down as their brain caused convulsions. Horrific pain would be present. Both had thrown up all over the floor and were foaming heavily at the mouth. However, as Charles discovered, they were still breathing.

Now he would have to finish the job himself. Wasn't that usually the case? Starting with Budge, he took a pillow, pressed it heavily over his face, and smothered him. When he removed the pillow, nine-year-old Budge was no longer breathing.

Moving to the other unconscious boy across the room, Charles put the pillow over his little face. He held it on six-year-old Amos until he was sure the boy was no longer breathing.

Now that the easy stuff was over, Charles sat down at the table to think through the rest of his plan. He had gone over it many times in his head and this part was going to be sweet.

First, he needed write a letter to Nettie. He had to make sure no one would blame her for any of the things he was about to do. When the letter was finished, he left it on the table making it easy for her to find.

Now that it was completely dark outside, he picked up Budge's body, walked over a half mile past the old house and across Frank Gamm's property line and laid the boy in the Gamm orchard. Repeating the trip, he laid little Amos' body beside his brother and covered them both with a blanket.

Gamm wanted his kids? Fine, he could have them. But he had a better ending for his meddling neighbor, coming up.

Back on his own property, he headed for the barn. As everyone knew, when a man's barn caught fire, everyone came running to help put it out. A man's barn was his livelihood and neighbors helped each other. That was what neighbors did.

To come running to help was exactly what Charles wanted them to do. He had planned what he called "the largest funeral in the State of Kansas," and that would include all of his enemies who wanted him to go to jail.

Charles was ready with his plan. He thought he might have been ready for this night all his life. After setting fire to the granary where the chickens roosted, he then torched several parts of the barn to accomplish the largest blaze possible.

He then sat a ways back with several rifles, loaded and ready to pick off all those people he had hated for so long. He felt he could rid the world of at least fifteen of those people as they rode in to help put out the fire. Now *that* would feel good. His position in the dark would make it very hard to see him or to shoot back. And he had enough firepower to drop them all.

The barn blaze provided a bright and eerie light in the night sky. Flames and smoke rose as high as a person could see. Charles sat waiting for what seemed like an hour. Fully engulfed, the barn had little chance of redemption even if an army showed up to help. *Where is everyone?* So far, not a soul had seen the fire. On the other hand, *had* they?

It slowly dawned on Charles that no one was going to help save his barn. Of course they had seen it, but they didn't *care*. The realization that his devious plan had backfired and he was unable to massacre his enemies made him crazy with rage.

Those lily-livered, dirt-sucking swine! They would let my barn burn down! It was more of a statement than a question. He was livid. If he had wanted to gun them down earlier, it was nothing compared to what he was feeling now.

His mind darting back and forth, he knew he had to rearrange his plans. Okay, Nettie was away and safe, part one done. The boys were out in Gamm's orchard, part two done. The barn was set on fire, but part three had been ignored and didn't work out as planned. It was time to move on to the rest of his evil plan.

Charles chained the handle of the water pump to the windmill so it would be useless to stop a fire if anyone actually wanted to. He made the trek to the old storage shed in the back of his property. With a shovel, he dug up the human bones he knew would be there. He gathered them up and hauled them back to the old house in a bag.

In the old house, Charles pulled the button off his pants that Nettie had sewn on for him, just this morning. He tossed it on the floor. He laid the human bones on the floor in the center of the house, arranging them like a body. After firing a shot from his old gun, he tossed it down with the bones. Pulling a knife out of his pocket, he threw it toward the gun.

Removing a rug, he flipped open a piece of the floor, and got out his many bags of gold. Charles left about ten thousand or so behind for his Nettie, plus what she had taken when she left. He placed the rest by the front door.

Going through the house one last time, he made sure all the pieces were in place. His last movement was to throw a bunch of bullets all over the floor of the old house. His job here was done.

Stepping outside with his gold, Charles proceeded to set the old house on fire. Like the barn, this one needed to completely burn down, so he made sure to set all four sides ablaze.

There was no emotion on Charles' face. He moved automatically and with purpose. He stood to watch the house burn. With red-orange flames flickering in his dead eyes, he knew it was almost over. There was only one thing left to do and his plan would be complete.

CHAPTER TWENTY-NINE

Saturday, January 21, 1905, finally ended and gave way to a new day. Throughout the night, much of the county watched the fires burning in the sky, and those nearest heard gunshots exploding every few minutes. By the dawn of Sunday, January 22, it was over.

Deadly quiet. And over.

Sunday morning, several people went to the sheriff with stories of the fires and gunshots. It was time to find out what was going on.

Sheriff Gleason took a handful of armed men and rode out to the Tuxhorn farm to investigate the stories surrounding all the commotion. The barn and old house had burned, all right, but no one seemed to be there.

Searching the destroyed premises went on for over an hour before the news came back to the sheriff. A deputy reported two small bodies found in Gamm's orchard. No one doubted their identities. The bodies of little Amos and Budge Tuxhorn had been found.

The news of the dead boys whirled around the sheriff's head while pain crashed in on him. He staggered to the nearest tree, where he was unable to keep down the big breakfast his wife had made before she went to church.

Those little boys! Dear God in Heaven, he killed those little boys! Sheriff Gleason and his men couldn't get their brains around it. All were stunned into silence as they surveyed the rubble around them.

The screaming, crying, and begging of Mary and Blaine was pounding in his head. *They knew he would do it. They knew he would! They knew. Why didn't he know it? Why didn't he come out and get those kids?*

After losing his stomach behind the tree, Gleason slid down the trunk onto the ground, crying. He didn't even care if any of his men saw him fall apart. As it turned out, he didn't have to worry, because several of his men did the same. The heart-wrenching wails of the distraught men were heard only by the ruins surrounding them. It was some time before they were able to return to work.

Three men were sent back into town for the doctor and coroner. One went to all of the churches, interrupting services to announce the gruesome discovery.

Churches emptied after the announcement. The men, still in their Sunday clothes, left the women to ride out and help in any way they could. Women cried while clinging to their children, not able to comprehend murdering your own.

When he arrived at the scene, John Friesen told the sheriff he saw the fire. He had climbed up onto his windmill to watch, but had been too afraid to go to Tuxhorn's in the middle of the night. It didn't take long to realize his fear had saved his life.

Frank Gamm had someone else to thank for his survival. He always stood up to the hateful Tuxhorn, but he probably would have gone to try and save the barn, for the kids' sake, if nothing else.

However, for some inexplicable reason, he and *his entire family* fell into a deep sleep and *no one* woke up to the ruckus on his neighbor's farm. Frank knew God had kept him asleep to keep him alive. No one would ever convince him otherwise. Then again, no one was trying.

Nothing of the barn remained. Charles had done a very good job of setting it on fire. They found three cats huddled in a corner that could find no way out. The granary was also history, and most of the chickens perished in the blaze.

The old house was not as devastated. In it, they found the button that Nettie said she had sewn onto Charles' pants just the day before. There was also a knife and gun that Blaine identified as belonging to his father. One bullet had been discharged from the gun and the rest blew up in the fire. Some bones were even found in the charred remains, but therein laid a controversy.

At first, they assumed the bones belonged to Charles. He torched the house and then shot himself. Pure and simple. What they were not taking into account was Charles, himself. Nothing he did was pure *or* simple.

The bones were white and cleaned of any flesh, plus there were not enough bones to make a full body. The skull was missing. Then, the coroner said it was not Charles Tuxhorn.

The county was divided in half. Some said they were his bones in the fire and others said he was still out there and were afraid for their very lives. Rumors went from probable to ridiculous. Everyone wanted to believe he was dead, but the evidence wouldn't support it.

First, Dr. Blake tried to explain there was no way all the flesh would be consumed by the fire. It was just not possible. Secondly, the unburned bones were cleaned white, with no flesh of any kind attached. And finally, if it was Charles, his whole body would be there, and it wasn't. Besides the skull, one leg and one arm could not be located.

"What more do you need, Sheriff? The man *isn't* dead. He has tried to make it look like he is, but Tuxhorn isn't here." Dr. Blake was getting more and more frustrated with the sheriff.

Sheriff Gleason already had the burden of guilt over the boys and Dr. Blake could understand his *wanting* Tuxhorn to be dead. *Everyone* wanted him dead. But the ugly truth was, it just didn't happen. He was out there somewhere, still alive.

"He's still alive." Dr. Blake had to say it one more time to make sure the sheriff was listening. He had said it many times already.

"I *get* it, Doc!" the sheriff yelled, as his frustrations exploded. He wasn't sure he could face people any more.

After refusing to remove the boys from the farm, he now had to face people with the results of that decision. How could he deal with them when he couldn't deal with himself? After recovering from the initial grief at the crime scene, he went on to gather as much information as he could. As he worked, he prayed, "Lord, please let him be dead. Please!"

But, he could no longer hang onto the belief Tuxhorn was dead. It wasn't possible. As much as the sheriff wanted it to be so, it just wasn't possible.

Money was missing from the burned out farm, too. About $11,000 in all was found. After his liquidation last week, there was no doubt, he had at least $30,000. Where was the rest of the money? Where was the gold he cherished so much? Only about $2,000 of the found money, was in gold. That was not Charles Tuxhorn at all. What happened to all that gold he had only days ago?

If Charles got away, whose bones were those? Most of the neighbors thought they must be the missing son, Edward. It obviously didn't bother Tuxhorn to kill his own, so what really had happened to him?

Like the barn burning, it was all beginning to look like a set up. But dead or alive, rumors spread from one end of the United States to the other. People were frightened out of their minds and knew, in their hearts, Charles was coming back to kill them all. They had reason to worry.

Newspapers ran the story from the limited information they were given.

A FIENDISH CRIME – TWO CHILDREN KILLED LAST SUNDAY

FATHER A MURDERER

CHILDREN MURDERED—MYSTERIOUS DISAPPEARANCE OF CHARLES TUXHORN

From New York to Washington State, the news of the Kansas murders made front page. Some reported Charles missing, some said he shot himself in the burning house. Without precedence, McPherson County, Kansas, was in shock for months.

Complete panic filled the county. Not knowing the whereabouts of Charles Tuxhorn, gun sales soared. The hardware stores couldn't restock fast enough.

One man went to Kansas City and bought up every gun he could get his hands on and brought them back. If a person proved financial hardship, a gun was loaned to them until this killer could be caught. No one was left unprotected.

All businesses in the surrounding cities of Inman and McPherson immediately started closing early. Whether owner or hired help, all people were home and off the streets before dark. After the sun went down, they knew Charles could get to any of them.

Home from work, husbands sat by their doors with loaded pistols throughout the evening in case Tuxhorn tried to break in. Loaded guns laid beside any person trying to sleep. On farms, hired help was rotated on guard duty so everyone could get a minimum of sleep.

School was suspended for the safety of all the children. If Charles would kill his own children, there was no doubt he would take the lives of those his enemies loved best. They couldn't, and wouldn't, take that chance.

Wives were armed for their own protection, as well as that of their children, during the day while their husbands worked. Children were not allowed to play outside or be out of the sight of a parent.

All church services were postponed in case of an attack on the community. By walking into a church, Charles could satisfy his revenge by killing parents and children. No one was going to set their family up to be annihilated by a lunatic.

The entire county came to a sudden stop.

~~~

The day the bodies were found, Nettie remembered the three letters Charles had given her to post while she was in town. She turned them over to the sheriff. Those letters became fuel to the already enormous bonfire of fear and gossip enveloping everyone's lives.

On the table in their new house, was the letter Charles had written to Nettie, herself. The following is his letter:

Saturday at 5 o'clock in the evening, January 21, 1905.

Dear Nettie,

I will try and write you a few lines to let you know what we have been doing since you left. We have been going out every time we see somebody coming on the road. Helderbrant came by first and old Slaback at five o'clock. Frank Gamm's brother-in-law came by. You know who I mean. I cannot think of his name now. He drives a grey team just the same. And I talked to your father just before dark and he seen us all. I do this so you can prove they seen the children after you left. It is dark now and I have to do something else now.

Well, Nettie I talked to your father about staying at his place. He said he had never said you could not come. He said you could come as far as he knows. Well Nettie it seems awful hard to do something I have never approved of. I want to do what is right but the court will not let me so I will close. Take good care of yourself and baby. So goodbye Love.

Charles H Tuxhorn to his wife Nettie Tuxhorn.

The first letter to be mailed was addressed to his oldest child, Bertha Tuxhorn, who lived in Springfield, Illinois. The original contents of this letter were too vile and violent to ever publish. A court officer read the following statement, while standing on the courthouse steps. It was the only statement ever allowed to be revealed to the public:

> In the letter to his daughter, she is accused, along with several of Tuxhorn's neighbors, of being responsible for the trouble between himself and the children. This seemed to be quite a stretch, since Bertha had let it be known about his beatings when she left home with Tilly, but had not made any contact with the family or the neighbors since leaving.
>
> He speaks disparagingly of her character and states that he never had any pleasure while married to her mother. He also stated she would get to "attend one of the largest funerals ever held in Kansas."

He professed his present wife had always been good to the children and that Bertha, along with others, had misrepresented the treatment they had received at his hands. He also stated that he had signed over all property to his current wife so that no child by Eva would receive one cent. If Bertha were to ever come back to the farm, she would be arrested for trespassing.

The other two letters were to his attorney, F.P. Hettinger, and a man he had done business with in McPherson, Mr. B. Harms. To these, he spoke kindly and expressed his innocence of all charges. He did not believe he would get a fair trial and again mentioned he planned to cause the largest funeral in Kansas. He further assured them he was in his right mind.

The coroner now had the law on his side when the sheriff announced Tuxhorn did not die in the fire. The bones did not belong to him. The Pinkerton Detective Agency was called in to find Charles Tuxhorn.

Pinkerton Government Services, Inc., founded as the Pinkerton National Detective Agency, was a private security guard and detective agency established in the United States by Allan Pinkerton in 1850.

Pinkerton became famous when he claimed to have foiled a plot to assassinate President-elect, Abraham Lincoln, who later hired Pinkerton agents for his personal security during the Civil War. Pinkerton's agents performed services ranging from security guarding to private military contracting work. At its height, the Pinkerton National Detective Agency employed more agents than there were members of the standing Army of the United States of America.

Armed with a photo, dozens of Pinkerton agents spread throughout the United States and Mexico in order to find Charles Tuxhorn. Attempts were made to find him in Europe, as well, but to no avail.

Belief in the fact he was still alive somewhere was widespread. Those close to the family and the law knew he didn't die in the fire, but where did he go?

Some say Pinkerton never found Charles. Some say an agent might have found him, but was paid off with some of the massive amounts of missing gold. Some don't have a clue either way.

What people did know was the fact they would not be attending the largest funeral in the state of Kansas. But they would attend the saddest.

CHAPTER THIRTY

Bertha Tuxhorn walked into Tilly's room on January 23, 1905. It was a bitter cold Monday morning. In fact, Springfield, Illinois, would break more than one record for cold that winter. The girls, however, felt the budding rainbow of color each spring always outweighed the bleak winters.

They lived in dorm rooms supplied by their employer, Concordia College, in Springfield. Tilly was folding laundry and putting it away before leaving for work.

Matilda Tuxhorn, now sixteen, was a beautiful person inside and out, at least to Bertha, she was. It was obvious to her why Momma wanted to get her out of that house and keep her safe. She was gentle and kind. Blonde and blue eyed, Tilly just couldn't see the evil in anyone or thing. Now her big sister would have to show her.

Settling in Springfield was the best place they could have found. It was a booming college town with young people from several states working for their degree. Concordia College was the sister college to Concordia Theological Seminary in

MURDER IS A FAMILY AFFAIR

Springfield, a Lutheran based school, which produced many outstanding ministers.

Since arriving in Springfield, they were both blessed with jobs at the college. While cleaning up schoolrooms after they let out, the girls were allowed to attend classes free. They couldn't get enough of the free education they were handed. Tilly would joke they were like wheat sucking up the summer rain.

With their hard work and increased education, Tilly was now a teacher's assistant. Bertha, at twenty-two, was working toward a degree in school administration. Life could not be more different from their roots.

Just when it seemed their childhood misery was behind them, this had to happen. Yes, they had heard about baby Henry, then Momma dying shortly after. That was when Bertha told Tilly how their Momma had insisted she take her when she left. Bertha missed her so much. Why was life so painful? Now she had to tell Tilly the most recent bad news.

"Tilly, I need to talk to you. Please sit down." Bertha kept her voice calm. She didn't want to frighten her sister unnecessarily.

"Sure, Bertha. Did that boy ask you out?" Tilly loved teasing about the men who watched them walk down the street. Bertha didn't smile at the comment.

"Tilly, it's in the paper." Bertha just had to get it out. There was no need to prolong it. "It's in the paper. Poppa killed Amos and Budge." Bertha's heart was breaking, but now was not the time to be weak. Tilly would need her.

Tilly stared at her for a few seconds. The look on her face told of her inability to take the horror in.

She saw the newspaper Bertha was holding by her side. She grabbed and opened it. The headlines were out of her old nightmares. Her little brothers were dead at the hands of their father.

"Bertha, nooooo!" Tilly wasn't strong like Bertha. Some things were just more than she could take.

Bertha held her and they cried in each other's arms for over two hours. When they were exhausted, Bertha told her sister they would have to make plans to go to the funeral. They would finally have a chance to visit Momma's grave, also. When they last saw Amos he was one year old and Budge was five.

"What kind of person could do this, Bertha?"

Bertha knew. Poppa was the most evil man she had ever met. He was certainly the kind of person who could do this.

They were able to get a train into McPherson the following morning, arriving late afternoon Tuesday, January 24, 1905. Going on into Inman, they were reunited with Mary and Blaine.

Left alone for hours, they talked about all that had happened. At first, Mary was mad at Bertha for leaving her to care for the little ones.

"I am so sorry, Mary. I couldn't take any more. You know he had a special hate for me. I have no idea why. I would have come and got you, but Poppa would never have let you go." Bertha shivered at the thought of his rage.

Mary said, "Yeah. I guess. But it was so hard and the boys were so little. After Momma died and Poppa took up with that harlot..."

"Mary, stop it." Blaine's heartbreak over the murder of his brothers was still raw and he couldn't stand any bickering. Not now.

Mary stared at him, knowing he shared the incredible pain she did. She walked over to him and put her arms around him. For a moment, the shared heartbreak was enough to keep them going.

Bertha and Tilly didn't say anything. They, too, hurt over the loss of Amos and Budge, but they both knew it wasn't the same pain Mary and Blaine had to deal with. They had begged for the little ones to be saved. Had they been adults, someone probably would have listened to them, but not the voice of children. It was surprising enough the law believed the abuse before they were all dead.

"We have to stick together to get through this funeral." Bertha meant what she said, and the rest agreed.

The hotel owner refused to let them pay and set them up in adjoining rooms. They could continue to visit as long into the night as they wanted.

~~~

It was Wednesday morning, January 25, 1905. Twenty-one-year-old Edward Tuxhorn ran into his employer's office in Lincoln, Kansas. He was crying and waving a newspaper.

His employer, David Cooper, grabbed the paper out of his hand. Edward then fell to the floor, sobbing.

After reading the headlines, David could see why he had fallen apart. He knew some about Edward's childhood and how he had to leave his young siblings, but this was unbelievable.

"Get your things together, Edward; we can be in Inman by nightfall. I'll go with you," Cooper said. He could hardly believe what he read. He didn't usually get involved with his employees' problems, but there was no way he would leave the young man to face this alone.

~~~

It was indeed dark when they finally arrived. They headed straight for the Sheriff's Office. Edward confirmed all the horror stories Mary and Blaine had told about their abuse and added a few of his own.

The sheriff told Edward they had thought the bones found in the house might have been his because no one had heard from him again.

"Why did you leave without saying a word? We all thought you were dead," Sheriff Gleason asked.

"I would have been if I'd stayed. I didn't just leave, Sheriff. Poppa told me if I was found on his property thirty minutes later, he would kill me dead. I think you know by now, what I knew back then—he meant it." Edward was reliving that last morning with his father and it was making him shake.

"We had a bad argument and we were about in a physical fight. Man, I was so tired of being beat that I was prepared to take him on. I was really going to beat the crap out of him and I told him so. I figured if I won, he couldn't hit me no more."

Taking a choked breath, he continued. "That's when he stopped suddenly and just looked at me real strange. I think Poppa said "I'm not August." But he could have said "it isn't August." I have no idea what that month had to do with anything, 'cause it was only February. He was talking crazy, and I wasn't going to wait around for a bullet to find me. He told me I had to leave right then or he would kill me, and I knew he meant it." There was fear in Edward's eyes as he went back through the events of that morning

"He wouldn't let me even go home for my clothes. He said get lost and never come back, so I did. I never got to say goodbye to Momma or anyone."

Sheriff Gleason nodded, not sure if Tuxhorn *ever* did anything that made sense. "Let's get you a room next to your family. The funeral is tomorrow afternoon."

It was the first Edward had heard about his siblings, but was glad to go along with the sheriff.

He didn't really know what to expect when he knocked on their door, but one thing he did know for sure, Budge and Amos wouldn't be there.

Mary opened the door and yelled to the others, "It's Edward!"

She threw her arms around him. Edward hugged her back while smiling at the others. They all talked for hours. It was very late by the time all had caught up with what had been happening with everyone else. It was time to get some sleep. Tomorrow would be a long and terrible day.

~~~

Thursday, January 26, 1905, started with the threat of a winter storm. However, by noon, dark clouds had retreated and the sun was shining. At two in the afternoon, Reverend Danks led the funeral in the Methodist church of Inman.

The crowd of people was staggering. People even came from other states to pay homage to the little boys. A large choir and an organist supplied music and several young boys served as pallbearers. There wasn't a time during the service that one couldn't hear the heartbreaking tears of people who just couldn't handle the horror of it all.

At the Inman cemetery, where Eva and her son Henry were buried, they laid to rest Amos and Budge.

It was not the largest funeral ever held in Kansas, as Charles had so desperately wanted it to play out. This was not the service for ten or fifteen valiant men who had attempted to save a man's barn from burning only to be murdered upon entering the property.

But with hundreds of people crowded into the cemetery, it was the largest funeral ever held in McPherson County, Kansas.

CHAPTER THIRTY-ONE

It was an incredibly beautiful day. The sunshine and warm temperatures made a man's heart sing. Well, maybe not sing, but happy, anyway. It had been a long ride and his horse was old and tired. He figured to buy a new one up ahead when this one no longer served his purpose.

Of course, he had seen an automobile or two in his travels. Plain silly, if anyone would ask him. The last automobile he saw was broke down, stranding two folks outside of town. He tipped his hat at them and kept right on riding. Any fool knew a horse was the only reliable way to get around.

Up ahead, he saw the beginnings of Camp Verde, Arizona. It used to be a government military fort, but not anymore. It closed up shop in 1890. The town was small but growing out around the camp itself. That could only mean he wasn't too far from his destination of Prescott, Arizona.

Prescott was booming. He had done his homework and learned gold had been discovered way back in 1838 and again in 1861. It caught the attention of Abe Lincoln, United States president at the time. He was looking for possible sources of funding for the North during the Civil War and so he created the Arizona Territory in 1864. In order to do this, President Lincoln removed Arizona from the New Mexico Territory.

The reason they had to be separated was simple. Lincoln didn't want Confederate sympathizers interfering. He appointed John Goodwin as the first territorial governor and Prescott as the first territorial capital. Located far enough north, a political conflict would be unlikely. A military attachment was sent to the newly established Fort Whipple, right next to Prescott.

Prescott lost the title of capital to Tucson in 1867, when Andrew Johnson was president of the United States, but gained it back in 1877. It was lost for the final time in 1889 to Phoenix.

That information didn't concern this cowboy near as much as the fact that Prescott was home to more than forty saloons for the enjoyment of the miners, cowboys, gunfighters, gamblers, and settlers that lived there. It sounded like a fun town.

It was close to noon and Camp Verde was just ahead. The man had to get his head on straight before riding in.

"Okay. You are not the old man—you are the new man. Remember that." The fact of the matter was he didn't look like the old man either. His hair was growing over his ears, looking shaggy and unkempt. The beard was showing some gray. His clothes were old and cheap, not much to his liking at all. The old horse was loaded down with gold.

After riding into town, he stopped at the livery.

"How far to Preston?"

"You can make it by nightfall if you want." The old livery man didn't even look up from the horseshoe he was scraping on.

He jumped off his horse and headed straight for the livery with his hand out.

"Hello, friend. My name is Johnson Thomas Chesterfield. I know it is a long name, but you can call me J.T., all my friends do. I am a preacher traveling to Prescott to do God's work. It's very nice to meet you, sir."

The old man seemed taken aback by the goofy grin on the preacher's face. He shook his hand and said, "Name's Bart. Bart Mason. I'm the livery here."

He looked J.T. over from top to bottom and added, "You sure could use some better clothes. I guess God's Work doesn't pay very well."

"No, sir, it don't. But I would rather preach the Good Word than do anything else. I'm headed for Prescott. I hear they need someone to preach to those sinners." The new J.T. grinned like an idiot.

"I imagine they could." Bart had to chuckle.

"Thank you much." J.T. got back on his horse and rode on out of town. He was back on the road toward Prescott and expected to be there by nightfall.

He was a bit amused to think of his new identity. He thought he had pulled that off pretty well. The man he hated so much—a preacher, of all things. What was it now, one, maybe two years since it all happened? Time really did go fast...

~~~

The idea came to him as payback for that stupid preacher making a fool of him in town. He had gone back the following day and found him at the stables.

J.T. was really frightened at first sight of Tuxhorn, but when Charles smiled and waved for him to come around back, he did. Charles put on his most charming self. He apologized profusely for the incident. He claimed he had been surprised when someone walked up behind him. He offered to pay for any medical expenses due to the broken fingers.

"Why, now, that's alright, Mr. Tuxhorn. I can see how you might have taken that wrong. Apology accepted." J.T. was thrilled at how this had all worked out. Tuxhorn had a temper, but obviously he wasn't completely a bad sort.

"Well, I know you don't know much about me, J.T., but I want to make all of this up to you. You said you were leaving for Arizona soon, that right? And call me Charles." He was on one of his 'get revenge' trips.

"Yes, sir...*Charles.* I am headed for Prescott, Arizona. There's a lot of gambling and drinking there, plus a lot of loose women. I am going to see if I can change that. The Lord will guide my way." J.T. loved talking about his plans. He knew in his heart, lives were going to change.

"I certainly understand how you would want to go there. Could I just ask a small favor of you before you go? I am willing to pay well for your help. How's ten dollars a week sound?" Charles had laid the trap.

J.T. thought that sounded just fine. The Lord knew he could use some new clothes for the rest of his trip. But he became concerned about the favor.

"Charles, I haven't seen ten dollars a week in my whole life. I can't imagine what I could do to earn that."

"It's easy, J.T. Exactly what you are doing right now, only just for me. You see, I never knew much about the Bible. My parents weren't God-fearing, like you are. I will pay you to come stay with me for a couple of weeks and teach me all about what the Bible says." Charles' face held the calm, charming demeanor he wanted, but inside he wanted to throw up.

He continued, "My wife is a God-loving woman and she wants most of all for me to be that kind of husband. So I want to surprise her after I learn all about it.

"Why, sure. I would love to do that. At least, what I can do in that short amount of time. But I don't need to impose upon your hospitality. You can meet me here in town. What time is good for you?" J.T. couldn't believe his good luck. The money would help make the trip a whole lot easier, and he would certainly have more food in his saddlebags.

"See, that's the thing. I can't come into town every day, being a farmer and all. You would have to come out to my farm. And since this is going to be a surprise, you couldn't tell anyone, not even anyone in town. As a preacher, you know how people gossip." It even sounded sincere to Charles.

"I have this shack out on the back side of my property. Oh, it's small, but I have fixed it up real nice and you would be very comfortable there. I could come by every day and you could teach me. You also would get to share the wonderful meals my wife cooks up. It would all be free, not like you are here in town, plus the money. What do you say?" Charles was finished. He knew it would be no problem to tell Nettie he was taking a meal out to a hand that he had working late.

J.T. thought it a bit odd, but ten dollars a week for teaching one pupil was certainly good wages. Free room and board, too. He would have plenty of time to read the Bible while he was alone.

"Fine. I'll do it. When do you want me to start?" J.T. was so excited.

"I'll meet you out of town by the old well on Friday around noon. Pack up everything you have, 'cause then you can just head out for Arizona from there. How's that?"

The deal was made. That afternoon J.T. let everyone know he was off to Arizona on Friday.

Riding along the trail, Charles was now watching the sun to see what kind of progress he was making toward Prescott. *Probably ought to push this old nag a little.* It was going to be dog meat soon enough, anyway.

He was thinking about that first day in the shack. In order to keep him there, he had moved his nice furniture in from the barn. He knew he had to make him comfortable. It worked. When J.T. first saw inside, he was very impressed by the quality of his room.

"Why, Charles! This is nicer than my hotel room. I appreciate it." J.T. couldn't believe his good luck.

Charles showed him the creek nearby for washing up, but warned him not to come out of the shack unless it was dark. No one could see him or it would spoil the surprise. J.T. was really into this game now, and promised to stay hidden.

The first week went well. Charles spent as much time as he could without raising questions from his hired help. J.T. was actually a good teacher, even though the subject matter wasn't something that could stir Charles. They took turns reading the Bible, and then J.T. would explain the story in terms Charles could understand.

When they were not discussing the Bible, Charles asked all about his family, like where he was from? Had he ever married? Did he have any children? When did he become a preacher? The questions were endless, but poor J.T. didn't notice. He thought they were friends sharing everything. However, Charles wasn't sharing, he was learning.

J.T. was getting cabin fever by the second week, but he managed to fill his end of the deal. The day before his tutorage was to end, he was getting excited about leaving.

"I have really enjoyed helping you out, Charles, but I gotta say I am really looking forward to being out in the fresh air again. This hiding out is a little strange." J.T. was a happy man. Twenty dollars was coming his way and Prescott was in front of him.

Charles said, "I don't blame you a bit, J.T. Thank you for all your help. There is one more thing I want to do for you before you leave. I want you to take off those old clothes, and I will get my wife to wash them up for you. That is no way to start a trip. You smell like a coon, my friend. Tonight you can slip down to the creek and take a bath. In the morning, I will bring you the money I owe you and your clean clothes."

J.T. laughed out loud and Charles joined in.

"Well, if that don't beat all. You are quite the host, Charles," J.T. said. He stripped down to his long johns and gave up the clothes. Charles left with a promise to come back early. And, in fact, it is one promise he was looking forward to keeping.

The following morning, before dawn Charles rode back to the shack. Freshly bathed, J.T. had his saddlebags packed and just needed his clothes. He ran out of the shack shouting "Good morning" when he saw Charles coming.

With the rising sun to his back, Charles was just a black shape riding up to the shack, so J.T. couldn't see his face. Another thing J.T. couldn't see was the bullet that went right between his eyes. He was dead before he hit the ground.

Stupid preacher. Charles was not the fool J.T. must have thought. *Ten dollars a week? In a pig's eye...*

As Charles planned, no one even knew the preacher was missing. They sure couldn't pin it on him. The shallow grave behind the shack was enough to cover the body from the hired help. The well-placed bullet in the face would keep anyone from recognizing who it was if the body was ever found.

The old clothes were folded and left under the bed, along with the saddlebags. He made sure anything belonging to J.T. was out of sight. J.T. had done a good job of cleaning up everything before his departure. No one would know he was ever there. Charles locked the shack from the outside and rode away.

He wanted the stupid man dead after humiliating him in town. But as it turned out, he served a bigger purpose. Charles needed a body for the fire and he needed a new identity. It must have been fate that brought the two of them together.

Riding into the glaring sun toward Prescott, he frowned when his thoughts took him back to the grave behind the shack. Digging it up to place the bones in the old house did not work quite as planned. Wolves had gotten to the shallow grave before he did. The whole body wasn't there and he couldn't even find the skull. No matter. He took what he had. The bones had been picked clean. *Guess when the wolves got through when him, the bugs got the rest.*

He slowed his horse a bit. He was pretty sure he saw some buildings in the distance. Prescott. It had to be.

"Okay, Johnson Thomas Chesterfield, it is time to start your new life. Will this old boy lead anyone to the Lord in this wicked town? Or will they end up making a sinner out of him?"

He laughed and rode on into his future.

EPILOGUE

Edward Tuxhorn lived three more years. In January of 1908, got into trouble with the law and committed suicide by drinking acid in order to avoid being sent to jail.

Bertha and Matilda returned to Illinois. They obtained their educations and both eventually married and had families.

Mary and Blaine stayed in Inman with a family who did everything in their power to show love to the children. Mary eventually married and stayed in the Inman, Kansas, area.

Blaine grew up to be an inventor of airplanes and their parts. He had his own flying school in Kansas City for many years and was highly regarded among his peers and community. He married and had a family.

Nine months after Charles murdered his sons, Netti gave birth to his twin girls. A year later she obtained a divorce from Charles for desertion. She remarried, sold the farm and all of her money was gambled or partied away. After her second divorce, she repented of her lifestyle, and eventually married a Mennonite man and lived a very strict religious life until her death in the early 1960s, at approximately 80 years of age.

~~~

Charles carried the violent temper and uncontrollable rage handed down from his grandfather to his father. Did it start there? No one can say.

Who received it from Charles? So many families can trace their bloodline back through a Tuxhorn somewhere in the past. What evil have their families had to live with?

What in the Tuxhorn blood has caused violence to thrive? Henry passed it to August, who passed it on to his son, Charles. But, how many other family members felt the same rage; or, did they simply pass it unknowingly to their own offspring?

There were suicides among August's children, as well as Charles.' There have been many suicides among his grandchildren and great-grandchildren, as well as severe depression and anger.

August and Charles both made front-page news all over the country with their horrific crimes. How many more went unnoticed, untold, or unknown?

I do not have all the answers, but I know evil is still among our family, waiting to make headlines again. And it will.

What happened when you went searching *your* family tree?

AUTHOR'S NOTES

I was adopted into the Tuxhorn family, however, I consider Raymond Lee Tuxhorn my dad, and I could not love him more. He married my mother, Blanche, when I was six and they had one child, Mike. I also have an older brother, Lou Duggan, loved by us all, along with his beautiful wife, Judy.

Charles and Nettie had a son, Clarence. Clarence had four children, one was my father, Raymond Lee. As you can see, this story hits *very* close to home. Charles and Nettie were Dad's grandparents.

In preparing to write this book, I spent years going through genealogy books, libraries, and websites. I have printouts from original newspaper accounts.

The story you have read is true, with the usual creative license to create conversations that probably did happen based on the resulting circumstances. Not all characters and events are real, but most are and have left a very heavy mark on our history.

~ Donalie Beltran

CHARLES TUXHORN

THIS IS CHARLES TUXHORN. HAS THIS FACE APPEARED IN YOUR FAMILY TREE? IF IT HAS, PLEASE CONTACT LINDA AT: lindahansel@yahoo.com

Made in the USA
San Bernardino, CA
13 January 2014